THE BATTLE OF FALLEN TIMBERS

A CHANGE OF WORLDS

DAVE WESTRICK

THE History PRESS

Published by The History Press
An imprint of Arcadia Publishing
Charleston, SC
www.historypress.com

First published 2025

Manufactured in the United States

ISBN 9781467159692

Library of Congress Control Number: 2025931879

Notice: The information in this book is true and complete to the best of our knowledge. It is offered without guarantee on the part of the author or The History Press. The author and The History Press disclaim all liability in connection with the use of this book.

There is no death. Only a change of worlds.
—Chief Seattle (Sealth), Suquamish Tribe

To Nanci,
my muse and editor-in-chief of my life

CONTENTS

ACKNOWLEDGEMENTS

More than twenty years ago, I became involved in the fight to save the Fallen Timbers Battlefield. One of the preservationist's strongest tools is education. Over the years, the Fallen Timbers Battlefield Preservation Commission and the Metroparks have organized hundreds of lectures, walks, tours, hikes and reenactments to promote the battlefield and to educate. I have been privileged to meet and work with some of the best minds, top scholars, and experts in the field of eighteenth-century American history.

In the course of two decades of activism, I've also grown to know many local history fans. The people who love history, regardless of their background or education, are the enthusiastic heart of what we do. Since the very first Fallen Timbers event I ever attended, there have been men and women who ask the questions and wait around until the event is over to talk to the speaker and share their passion. This book is a collection of character profiles, historical oddities and stories that will appeal to the dedicated history lover. If you've ever waited until the end of a talk and then approached the speaker with a thank-you or a story related to the topic, or if you've ever walked up to a famous writer or professor and said, "Did you know that…?"—this book is for you.

Special thanks to Dr. Shannon Hughes; Dr. G. Michael Pratt; Dr. Larry Nelson; Dr. Janet Rozick; Jessica Klimesh; Xavier Allen; Steve Madewell; Taylor Moyer; Kenneth Dickson; Dr. Mary Stockwell; Bill Hogeland; the late Dr. Ralph Johnson, curmudgeon extraordinaire; and my good friend the late Bruce Huddleston, who fought tirelessly to save the battlefield. "Bro, we got it done."

Dave Westrick
April 2024

INTRODUCTION

THE BATTLE OF FALLEN TIMBERS

It was a small fight in the wilderness. For the United States, it was the beginning of greatness, of a government that would eventually rule from coast to coast and of a military that would grow to win two World Wars and become the greatest fighting force on the planet. For the English, it was a stopping point, a wall, forever limiting imperial ambitions in North America. For the American Indians, it was the end of greatness and of the life their ancestors had led for thousands of years.

All this happened over two hundred years ago, on the outskirts of current day Maumee, Ohio. On a hot August morning, a coalition of a dozen divided Indian tribes faced a federal army raised to defend fifteen quarreling, fractious states. The battle lasted less than two hours, with fewer than one hundred killed. It was a small fight in the wilderness, but it changed the world forever.

Background

Following the end of the American Revolution, white settlers and land speculators began flooding into Ohio Country, causing conflict with the Native American tribes who lived there. The young American nation, under the leadership of President George Washington, attempted to suppress the Native resistance, but a coalition of tribes from the Ohio and Great

Charge of the Dragoons, by Rufus Zagbaum. *Harper's Weekly*, 1895. *Ohio History Connection.*

Lakes Region under the leadership of Little Turtle, Blue Jacket, Tarhe, Buckongahelas and other war leaders destroyed two military expeditions sent to subdue them.

The first expedition, under General Josiah Harmar, moved through western Ohio and Indiana to attack Miami Indian villages at what is now Fort Wayne, Indiana. After suffering heavy losses in several engagements, Harmar was forced to withdraw. In 1791, General Arthur St. Clair led a second expedition. Near what is now Fort Recovery, Ohio, the army was surrounded and destroyed. The Battle of the Wabash is still considered by many to be the greatest defeat ever suffered by the U.S. Army. The Americans suffered a 97 percent casualty rate. Some refer to the defeat as the Battle of a Thousand Slain.

Encouraged by the defeat of the U.S. forces, the British government sought to reassert its influence and built Fort Miamis in what was clearly U.S. territory. The fort (built in current-day Maumee, Ohio) was a message to the world that the new United States was not a country to be taken seriously.

Alarmed at the potential loss of the Northwest Territory, Washington appointed Major General Anthony Wayne to raise and train a professional United States army. Wayne's army, organized on the model of the Roman legions, began moving north from Cincinnati in late 1793, building a series of supporting forts as it went. The Miami, Shawnee, Ottawa, Wyandot, Delaware, Mohawk, Mingo, Potawatomi, Wea, Ojibwa and other tribes, supported by volunteer Canadian militia and rangers, opposed Wayne's advance.

THE BATTLE

It rained the morning of August 20, 1794, soaking everything. By ten o'clock, the sun was shining, and the landscape was steaming in ninety-degree heat. The American army, sweating in wool uniforms, marched up the river toward an area where a tornado had torn down a line of trees. In these fallen timbers, the Natives waited among rotting logs and the wet green undergrowth. The battle began when a mounted militia unit on Wayne's right flank encountered some of the estimated one thousand Indian warriors waiting to ambush. The militia came under heavy fire and were driven back. Some of the Indians broke cover and pursued. Initially, the legion's front guard stalled the Indian advance, and then they also began to fall back. Wayne's regulars formed up and pushed forward, pressing into the Indian line with fixed bayonets. After a period of close-quarter fighting, the Indians fell back. Wayne pursued for several miles into what is now Maumee, Ohio. Wayne then halted, regrouped his army and prepared for an Indian counterattack.

When the Indians did not counterattack, Wayne moved forward to Fort Miamis. Wayne and the fort commander, Major William Campbell, exchanged a series of tense letters and threats but avoided actual combat. After two days of taunting, Wayne withdrew, burning the Indian cornfields and villages behind him.

The battle left the Indian coalition defeated and the English authority humiliated. The following summer, representatives of the major tribes signed the Treaty of Greenville, giving up most of the Ohio Territory and many of their rights in the Great Lakes Region.

LEGACY OF THE BATTLE

Though casualties were light (around fifty dead on each side), the Battle of Fallen Timbers is considered one of the most decisive battles in U.S. history. Many historians rank it below only Gettysburg and Yorktown in importance.

For the United States, victory at Fallen Timbers made westward expansion possible. The creation of a professional army enabled Washington to build a strong central government, as opposed to a weak alliance of states. The battle secured the future states of Wisconsin, Michigan, Indiana, Illinois, Minnesota and Ohio and sealed the fate of the Native tribes living there. It also gave the former colonists a new identity as Americans.

For the British, the battle was a serious setback to their ambitions in North America. The Loyalist soldiers fighting alongside the Indians would start to think of themselves as Canadians, and the French fighting against the U.S. troops would soon realize that their future was with the Americans.

For the American Indians, the battle marked the loss of their lands, the beginning of forced removal and the end of tribal independence. When the story of the American Indian is told, the Trail of Tears really begins at Fallen Timbers.

It was a small fight in the wilderness, but it was a large change of worlds.

CHAPTER 1

THE DEFENDERS

The Native Americans

Little Turtle, Native American Napoleon

This story shall the good man teach his son,
And Crispin Crispian shall ne'er go by,
From this day to the ending of the world,
But we in it shall be remembered.
We few, we happy few, we band of brothers.
For he to-day that sheds his blood with me
Shall be my brother.
—*Shakespeare's* Henry V, *Act 4: Scene 3*

Henry's speech to his men on the eve of a battle in which they were outnumbered and not expected to win has become a staple in literature. It is especially popular in stories of warrior cultures. One version in a forgotten movie goes something like this: "Our people shall sing of this day, around their campfires, for a thousand years." It is a line fit for a legend.

Miami Chief Mihšihkinaahkwa (Me-she-kin-no-quah)—or, as the English called him, Little Turtle—was one such legend. Affable and easygoing, he was well-liked. But this nice guy was also one of the most successful battle tacticians in American history.

Born in what is today Indiana, Little Turtle lived on the Eel River not far from present-day Fort Wayne, Indiana. The British commander of Detroit, Colonel England, described Little Turtle as "the most decent, modest,

Left: Northwest Native American Confederacy, 1785–95. *Map by author.*

Opposite: Little Turtle. *U.S. Army Military History Institute. Artist unknown.*

sensible Indian I have ever conversed with."[1] But beneath that humble façade, Little Turtle was an uncommonly gifted war leader.

The Americans sent three separate armies to invade the Miami villages at the headwaters of the Maumee River. Despite being outnumbered every time, Little Turtle found a way to destroy each army. In 1780, a French adventurer named Augustin de La Balme occupied the Miami village called Kekionga (present-day Fort Wayne, Indiana) and set out to destroy Little Turtle's village on the Eel River. On the morning of November 5, Little Turtle surrounded the French force and attacked. La Balme and almost all his men were killed.

Ten years later, an American army under the command of General Josiah Harmar attacked Kekionga. Together with Blue Jacket of the Shawnee and members of several other tribes, the Miami engaged the Americans in several fights. The Natives' actions were well planned and well executed and left the American army shattered.

A year later, under the leadership of Arthur St. Clair, the Americans tried again. This time, things went even worse for them. The forces of Little Turtle, Blue Jacket, Buckongahelas and Tarhe surrounded a sleeping American camp and, on the morning of November 4, 1791, destroyed it. More than six hundred Americans were killed, and all but a few of the survivors were wounded. The American casualty rate was 97 percent. An unknown number of civilians were also killed. It is still considered the worst military defeat ever suffered by the U.S. Army. The Native forces, on the other hand, suffered only twenty-one dead. Some refer to this as the Battle of a Thousand Slain.

LITTLE TURTLE.

The fourth time the Americans came, Little Turtle had misgivings. Anthony Wayne's army was better trained, better organized and better led than the other American troops. It was also aimed not at the Miami heartland but at Detroit. In council with other tribes in August 1794, Little Turtle urged peace: "The Americans are now led by a chief who never sleeps." However, Blue Jacket and other tribal leaders overruled Little Turtle, and Little Turtle agreed he would follow their leadership. The day of the battle, he fought with his Miami warriors. Fallen Timbers was the only time Little Turtle ever experienced defeat in battle.

Following the battle, the rift between Little Turtle and Blue Jacket grew worse. After twenty years of war, Blue Jacket decided resistance was pointless and became the biggest advocate of the Treaty of Greenville. Little Turtle held out, but finally, in August 1795, he signed. According to legend, he said, "As I am the last to sign it, I will be the last to break it." In the following years, Little Turtle became an advocate for learning the white man's ways and assimilating. With his son-in-law, William Wells, Little Turtle made several trips to meet U.S. presidents and was active in trying to preserve the rights of the Miami.

Little Turtle opposed Tecumseh's attempts to resist white expansion, and his friendships with whites made him increasingly unpopular with his people. By the time of his death in 1812, Little Turtle had been removed from all positions of tribal authority. It was an unfortunate end to a life spent in service to his people.

Today Mihšihkinaahkwa is loved by his people and his many descendants. Some historians consider him a military genius and even refer to the Northwest Indian War as Little Turtle's War. Descendants and fans of Blue Jacket sometimes protest and cite evidence showing that Blue Jacket deserves as much credit as his more modest associate. What we do know is that when they worked together, they accomplished great things.

Perhaps someday there will be a movie made, and the two great war chiefs will stand on the site of St. Clair's defeat, looking around at the bloody snow and the remains of a once great army, and one will say, truthfully, "Our people will sing of what we did here today for a thousand years."

TOM LYONS OF THE LENAPE, MAN OF A THOUSAND STORIES

Reenactor Jeremy Moore. *Photo by author.*

Tom Lyons of the Leni Lenape (Delaware) people was a real man, not fictional, who fought at the Battle of Fallen Timbers. His Lenape name, Kaschates, translates simply to Tobacco. As an old man, he chose to live alone in what is today Holmes County and North Central Ohio, a place where he had frequent contact with White settlers and thus inspired thousands of tall tales. His descendants still live in the region. There are so many stories about Tom that it is hard to sort them out. He added to the confusion by occasionally telling tales to white people that weren't entirely accurate. To put it in today's slang, he sometimes liked to mess with people, knowing they would talk.

What we do know about Tom is that he was a warrior of the Lenape and fought in many battles over the course of a long life. He was born in what is today New Jersey. His band was forced out, though, and they lived for a time in Pennsylvania. It was in Pennsylvania that Tom came in contact with Amish settlers and learned to speak German in addition to the Algonquian language of the Lenape he already spoke. Tom later learned English as well. He fought in the French and Indian War and claimed to have participated in the Jacob Hochstetler cabin attack 1757. Some historians now doubt that Tom was there despite the fact that fifty years after the fact, Tom sometimes told the story in terrifying detail to Amish settlers. The Amish found it especially frightening because he would recall the screams of the dying in perfect German.

Tom fought with the Lenape during the American Revolution and was most likely present in 1782 when Colonel William Crawford was burned at the stake in retaliation for the massacre of Moravian (Christian) Delawares by American militia. Tom was never a Moravian.

Tom fought at the Battle of Fallen Timbers, and we have his first-person account, recorded in the 1880 *History of Ashland County*. White settler Allen Oliver recalled his conversation with Tom fifty years after the battle:

Allen Oliver: "You say you were at the battle with Wayne. What do you think of Wayne as a white chief?"

Tom Lyons: "Him be great chief. He be one devil to fight. Me hear his dinner horn—way over there go toot, toot; then way over here it go toot, toot—then way over other side, go toot toot. Then his soldiers run forward—shoot, shoot; then run among logs and brush. Indians have got to get out and run. Then come Long Knives with pistols and shoot, shoot. Indians run, no stop. Old Tom see too much fight to be trap—he run into woods—he run like devil—he keep run till he clear out of danger. Wayne great fight—brave white chief. He be one devil."

Mr. Lewis Oliver states that while "Old Tom" was going through this description of the fight, he gesticulated, grimaced and expressed as much emotion as if he had been in the midst of the battle. In fact, terror was evinced in the whole of the mimic battle he relived.

Tom's account fits very well with what we know of the battle. The militia units used horns to signal. From the sounds of horns and gunfire, the Lenape knew they were being flanked on both sides and had to fall back. What I am skeptical about, though, is the way Tom's speech was recorded by the white settlers. A man who spoke three languages probably did not sound like Tonto.

Some say Tom fought in the War of 1812. At that time, though, he would have been around seventy years old, so I think it is unlikely. As an old man, he lived alone in the woods of Holmes and Richland Counties and became an object of curiosity and fear as the "last Indian."

Tom became the subject of many myths, legends and lies. There are at least fifteen different stories detailing how one person or another murdered Tom Lyons, either for vengeance or simply because they wanted to be rid of him. There is actually a book by Robert A. Carter titled *Tom Lyons, The Indian Who Died Thirteen Times*. What is most likely true is that Lyons moved to a Delaware reservation elsewhere in Ohio, where he passed away of natural causes in 1824. He was fierce until the end. As an old man hunting and living alone, he was often subjected to harassment and threats. According to several accounts, his standard reply was, "I have taken ninety-nine white scalps; one hundred would be a nice even number. I like even numbers."

Tarhe and the Wyandot Sacrifice

In August 1794, twenty-one-year-old Jonathon Alder entered a small Wyandot village on the Sandusky River. Although white, Alder had been captured as a child and raised as a Native American. He was well known and trusted among the Ohio tribes. On this August day, he had a message from Tarhe, chief of the Wyandots. Tarhe's message was that the Wyandots were going to fight Wayne on the Maumee and he needed more men. So all the men of fighting age left with Alder. In total, twenty warriors left for Fallen Timbers, but only two returned.

The Battle of Fallen Timbers was devastating to the Wyandot people. We have no accurate number of Native Americans killed that day, but Wayne boasted of killing over two hundred. Modern historians put the number closer to fifty. Though we cannot know for sure, it appears that the majority of Native Americans who fell that day were Wyandots.

The Wyandots were led by Chief Tarhe, nicknamed the Crane by the French because he was exceptionally tall for the period (six foot four) and thin. Tarhe was born in 1742. He may have taken part in Braddock's Defeat in the French and Indian War, but this can't be verified. He supported the Ottawa leader Pontiac in Pontiac's War and Shawnee Chief Cornstalk in Lord Dunmore's War. Under Tarhe's leadership, the Wyandots became the fiercest enemy of the United States. They fought many engagements during the American Revolution and during the Northwest Indian War. Tarhe fought at Harmar's Defeat and participated in the destruction of St. Clair's army.

Many stories are told about the famous British Indian agent Simon Girty and his exploits in the Ohio Territory. What is seldom mentioned, however, is that under Tarhe's command, a group of Wyandot warriors often acted as Girty's bodyguard.

At the Battle of Fallen Timbers, the Wyandots were next to the Canadian militia on the Indians' right flank. When the Indian line collapsed, the Wyandots and Canadians covered the retreat at tremendous cost. Of thirteen Wyandot chiefs, all were killed except Tarhe, who was severely wounded when a musket ball smashed his right elbow.

After a lifetime of war, Tarhe decided it was time to make peace. Tarhe led his people to Greenville to sign the peace treaty. When he spoke to Wayne and the assembled U.S. and tribal representatives, he did so proudly, not as a defeated enemy but as a warrior tired of killing Americans. "Elder brother," he said, addressing the Americans, "I see you lying in a gore of blood. It is

Left: Tarhe, 1817. *Artist unknown.*

Right: Monument to Chief Tarhe in Wyandotte County, Ohio. *Photo by author.*

me, an Indian, who caused it. Our tomahawk yet remains in your head—the English gave it to me to place there. Elder brother, I now remove it."[2]

Once he had declared peace, Tarhe fought to keep it. For the rest of his life, he supported the United States. He opposed Tecumseh and supported the United States in the War of 1812. As a man of over seventy, he led a group of Wyandots in support of William Henry Harrison's invasion of Canada.

Tarhe died at the age of seventy-six near Upper Sandusky, Ohio. His funeral was the largest ever held for a Native American chief. Indian leaders from all over North America attended. Today, a stone monument marks the spot where it is believed he died. On a rural country road surrounded by a cornfield, the monument reads, "Tarhe, a Distinguished Wyandot Chief and Loyal American."

BLUE JACKET, LAST WAR CHIEF OF THE SHAWNEE

In May 1788, on the Kentucky frontier, a group of mounted Kentucky militiamen stumbled upon a small group of Shawnee warriors warming themselves by a fire they'd made in an old tree stump. A steady rain and high winds had soaked everyone to the bone. Guns were pointed and triggers pulled, but the wet powder failed to fire. In the confusion that followed, the Indians scrambled to get away on foot while mounted frontiersmen tried to kill or capture them. An unusually tall and broad-shouldered Indian dropped his musket and surrendered to the Kentuckians, allowing his companions to escape. The big Shawnee wore a black raven-skin cap with the wings spread out on either side of his head. In the pouring rain, he looked more like a figure from Norse mythology than a war chief of the Shawnee nation.

Weyapiersenwah ("the whirlpool")—or Blue Jacket, as he's more commonly known—was a larger-than-life figure. Even his capture is a legend. Beaten and mistreated, he still managed to persuade the frontiersmen not to kill him but to, instead, take him to see his old friend Daniel Boone. While bound, he was taken on a journey deep into the Kentucky settlements. The first night that the group stopped at Boone's tavern, though, Daniel was not there. Legend tells us that Blue Jacket and his captors engaged in a drinking contest and that after the last white man passed out, Blue Jacket stood up and walked home. But that's not exactly true. That morning found Blue Jacket passed out on the floor with the frontiersmen, all of them drunk.

The second night of the journey, Blue Jacket's hands and feet were tied, and he was left in a small building with a chain around his feet. Somehow, though, he got out of the chain, untied his feet and slipped past his sleeping guard. With no food or provisions and his hands tied behind his back, Blue Jacket managed to avoid the pursuing frontiersmen and their bloodhounds. Two weeks later, he arrived at an Indian village in Ohio, scratched from thornbushes, starving and bruised but still alive.

This story is classic Blue Jacket: negotiating for his life, then celebrating with his captors all night. It portrays Blue Jacket as a shrewd and successful businessman who traded with whites and Indians alike. The Indian warrior who escaped with his hands tied behind his back and fled through the woods was the same War Chief Blue Jacket who led more raids, fought in more battles and was responsible for the deaths of more white people than any Native American in history.

For twenty years, from the Battle of Point Pleasant in 1774 to the Battle of Fallen Timbers, Blue Jacket fought the white invaders. There were brief, intermittent periods of peace, but they never lasted. Like most tribes, the Shawnee attempted to remain neutral when war broke out between Great Britain and the colonies. That ended in November 1777 when a much-respected chief of the Shawnee, Cornstalk, was murdered in cold blood by an unruly group of frontiersmen. Following this, it is believed that Blue Jacket organized and led the first of many retaliatory raids.

Blue Jacket was always decisive. When peace was declared, he was the first to reestablish trading ties and open for business. When war broke out, he was the first to gather his forces and strike back. The struggle for the Old Northwest came to a head in 1790. Blue Jacket moved his village farther from the whites for safety and relocated near the Miami villages on the Eel and Maumee Rivers. Here began one of the great partnerships of history, between Blue Jacket and Little Turtle (Mihšihkinaahkwa) of the Miami. Later there would be friction and hard feelings between the two men, but for a while, they acted in harmony.

In October 1790, an American army led by General Josiah Harmar invaded the Miami homeland. In two battles, on October 19 and 21 respectively, the Native Americans successfully outmaneuvered, trapped and destroyed two companies of Harmar's men, and Harmar was forced to withdraw. Most historians give Little Turtle the credit for planning and leading this victory, but Blue Jacket was also leading and fighting. A year later, on November 4, 1791, a combined Indian force under Little Turtle and Blue Jacket destroyed another American army under the command of Arthur St. Clair. With over six hundred Americans left dead on the field and a 97 percent casualty rate, the Battle of the Wabash remains the worst defeat ever suffered by an American army.

After an unsuccessful attack on Fort Recovery during the summer of 1794, Little Turtle and Blue Jacket began to see things differently. In a meeting on August 18, Little Turtle strongly argued for making peace with Anthony

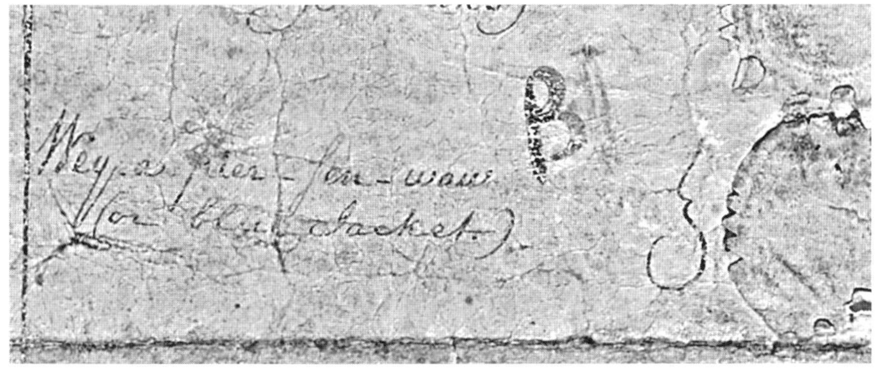

Weyapiersenwah's signature on the Greenville Treaty. A clerk spelled his name as it sounded; Blue Jacket then signed a large *B. Courtesy of the U.S. National Archives and Records Administration.*

Wayne, while Blue Jacket still believed they could defeat the Americans. With the backing of several other important chiefs, Blue Jacket carried the day. On the morning of August 20, Blue Jacket was in charge when the Northwest Indian Confederacy met Wayne's legion in the Battle of Fallen Timbers. Vastly outnumbered, the Confederacy was unable to stand up to Wayne's well-disciplined troops and was decisively defeated.

The winter of 1794–95 was a time of soul-searching for the Native Americans. After twenty years of resistance, Blue Jacket decided it was time to make peace. He led his people to Greenville and signed the treaty. In doing so, Blue Jacket gave away much of his power among the Shawnee. He was a war chief. In times of peace, though, the tribe is led by peace chiefs.

Blue Jacket spent his last years enjoying his life and, according to some, indulging his fondness for good food and drink. He also spent a great deal of time sharing his experiences in war and politics with a younger Shawnee named Tecumseh. Blue Jacket died of natural causes around 1810. Though Tecumseh and his followers fought in the War of 1812, the Shawnee as a people never declared war. Weyapiersenwah (Blue Jacket) was and is the last war chief of the Shawnee.

Buckongahelas of the Lenapi: "As Strong a Friend as I Was an Enemy"

Of the great Native American leaders of the Northwest Confederacy, Buckongahelas, chief of the Lenapi (Delaware), is probably the least familiar to non-Native people. Unlike Blue Jacket or Little Turtle, he did little business with whites. He did not have a white nickname or a simple English translation of his name. There are also very few legends or tall tales about him to recite or debunk. A quiet and intelligent man, he did not give historians a lot to work with.

What we do know, though, is that Buckongahelas fought in the French and Indian War, the American Revolution and the Northwest Indian War. He was seventy-four years old when he led his warriors at Fallen Timbers. White people were shocked by his appearance. He had pierced his earlobes and then stretched them until they rested on his shoulders. One earlobe was torn. According to one story, it was hit by a bullet during the Battle of Point Pleasant. Buckongahelas is described as a likable and easygoing person, beloved by his people. He was also a fierce war leader and an enemy of the American settlers.

Buckongahelas was born in the colony of Delaware, and he and his tribe were constantly pushed west by white settlers. He lived in current-day West Virginia until 1773, when a white settler murdered his son. For the next twenty-four years, Buckongahelas fought the Americans every opportunity he got.

In 1781, he visited a peaceful Delaware Christian village named Gnadenhutten. In an impassioned speech, which was recorded by John Heckewelder, a Moravian missionary, Buckongahelas implored his people to move farther west, where they would be safe. According to Heckewelder, "Eleven months after this speech was delivered by this prophetic chief, ninety-six of these same Christian Indians, about sixty of them women and children, were murdered at the place where these very words had been spoken, by the same men he had alluded to, and in the same manner that he had described."[3]

Blue Jacket sought Buckongahelas's counsel, and together with Little Turtle of the Miami, they formed the core of the Native Confederacy. Buckongahelas and his band of Lenape fought in every major battle. They were a key part of the great victory over Arthur St. Clair. Buckongahelas experienced one of his few defeats at the Battle of Fallen Timbers. The following year, he signed the Treaty of Greenville and promised to be as good a friend to the United States "as I have heretofore been an active enemy."[4]

Local legend claims that the town of Buckhannon, West Virginia, was named after Buckongahelas. In 2000, a statue of Buckongahelas holding his dying son Mahonegon was erected in the city park. According to legend, when his son died, Buckongahelas swore revenge on his killer, Captain William White. In 1927, a popular historical romance was written wherein Buckongahelas searches for years for his son's killer, but historians have disputed many of the details. What we know is that on March 8, 1782, nine years after the murder of Mahonegon, Captain William White died at the hands of an unidentified Native American man. Buckongahelas was also known as Petchnanalas, which means "fulfiller" or "one who succeeds in all he undertakes."

In his final years, Buckongahelas, war chief of the Lenape, lived near Muncie, Indiana, where he died of smallpox in 1805.

Egushawa of the Odawa:
A Life Spent in the Service of His People

Egushawa, also known as Egushaway or Augooshaway, was a chief of the Odawa. His name means "who brings together" in the Odawa language, and indeed, he was good at uniting his people. He was a diplomat, a force in the Northwest Indian Confederacy, and an experienced combat leader. Despite being around sixty-eight years old, he led his warriors in the heaviest fighting at Fallen Timbers. The Odawa were fighting next to the Wyandot and Canadian volunteers when the battle reached its climax. Intense fire from the advancing Americans decimated the Native line. Several Canadians were killed or wounded, Tarhe of the Wyandot was wounded and most of the Wyandot chiefs and their warriors fell. Egushawa and Little Otter of the Odawa were also severely hurt. Little Otter was shot through his body, so his warriors threw him over a horse and carried him off the field. Egushawa was shot in the face. Overwhelmed, the Indian line collapsed. If you were to dramatize the moment, it might sound like this:

> *We were driven back through the woods and swamps to the end of the hill, where the great Chief of the Ottawas, Turkeyfoot, exhorted the braves to stop and drive the pale face from our country....He stood upon a rock and called to the warriors to be brave and that the Great Spirit would make them strong. Suddenly his voice ceased, and he slid from the rock shot through the breast with a rifle ball and lay dying.*
> *—Kin-jo-i-no, an Ottawa, to Dresden Howard in the 1820s*[5]

Sounds great, except there is no rock where Egushawa fell, and in no way does Egushawa translate to "Turkeyfoot." Lastly, and importantly, Egushawa did not die. The tough old warrior was badly scarred and left with only one eye, but he survived.

Egushawa was born somewhere near Detroit. He fought in the French and Indian War and Pontiac's War. When Pontiac was killed, Egushawa became one of the principal (if not the principal) war chiefs of the Odawa. He fought against the Americans in the Battle of Oriskany; almost captured George Rogers Clark near Vincennes, Indiana; and opposed Daniel Boone at the Battle of Blue Licks.

Egushawa was not just a war leader. In his published journals, the British lieutenant governor of Detroit, Henry Hamilton, noted Egushawa's diplomatic skills and described him as "a sensible Indian, a considerate man, coolly brave but cautious of creating jealousy among the other nations." According to Hamilton, Egushawa was the most respected leader among the Great Lakes Tribes.

Egushawa was a leader of the Northwest Indian Confederacy and took part in the defeat of General Harmer and the total destruction of St. Clair's army in 1791. His losses at Fallen Timbers and the hard winter of 1794–95

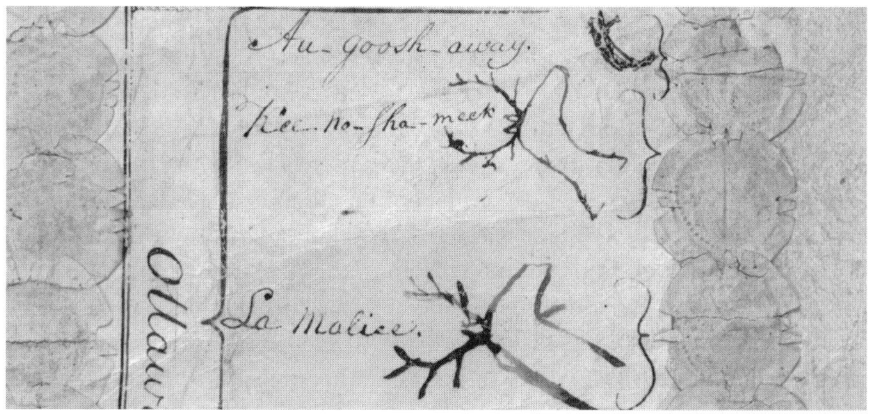

Eugushawa's mark on the Greenville Treaty: an otter (at the top). An American spelled his name Au-goosh-away. *Courtesy of the U.S. National Archives and Records Administration.*

changed everything, prompting Egushawa to lead his small, starving band to Greenville in the summer of 1795, where he signed the peace treaty.

The warrior diplomat still had one last act to play. At the Greenville treaty conference, the Americans used a standard trading trick. They gave the Indians more gifts or trade goods than they could carry, knowing the Indians would have to leave some of their "presents" behind, thereby allowing the whites to recover the stuff and regift it to the next group. Before leaving Greenville, the old, disfigured chief approached Anthony Wayne and, in all sincerity, asked where his boat was. Confused, Wayne asked his meaning, and Egushawa explained he would never want to insult the United States by leaving all this good stuff behind. Incredibly, Wayne ordered his soldiers to build a boat so that the Odawa could take all their presents home with them.

Egushawa died of natural causes a year later at the age of seventy. The fictional Chief Turkey Foot is remembered for the way he died. But Egushawa, his real-life counterpart, should be remembered for the way he lived.

Tecumseh: More Than a Legend

Tecumseh and Harrison: Enemies for Life

The morning of August 20, 1794, was a defining moment in the lives of two young men on opposite sides of the battlefield. William Henry Harrison of Virginia was a twenty-one-year-old aide to General Anthony Wayne.

Somewhere east of Wayne and Harrison's position, the Shawnee were engaging Wayne's regulars, and a warrior in his mid-twenties was in the midst of it. This warrior, Tecumseh, was relatively unknown, as he was not a chief, but he was in the fight.

The Battle of Fallen Timbers was an experience neither Harrison nor Tecumseh would ever forget, a turning point in their lives. Harrison used the experience as a résumé builder and embarked on an ambitious career as a politician and soldier that eventually led him to the White House.

On the other hand, Tecumseh, reflecting on his experience as part of a unified tribal confederacy, devoted his life to the idea of Native American unity and resistance to white expansion. As governor of the Indiana Territory, Harrison was aggressive in buying Indian land and pushing the Indians out. Tecumseh did his best to stop him. Harrison's accumulation of Indian land through negotiations and dealings with small village leaders and Tecumseh's work to unify the tribes put the two on a collision course.

Harrison and Tecumseh met twice, once in August 1810 and once in July 1811, in Vincennes, Indiana. In the first meeting, Tecumseh told Harrison bluntly, "I want the present boundary line to continue….Should you cross

A popular illustration of the meeting of Tecumseh and Harrison. Harrison's clothing may be the only thing close to accurate here. *John Reuben Chapin and William Ridgway (engraver), circa 1818.*

The Dying Tecumseh, Ferdinand Pettrich, 1854. *Smithsonian National Portrait Gallery. Photo by author.*

it…I assure you it will be productive of bad consequences." The meeting degenerated when Tecumseh's speech became more animated and one of the translators heard a threat and cocked a pistol. Weapons were drawn on both sides; Tecumseh drew a pipe tomahawk and Harrison his sword. Despite the tension, calm prevailed, and no blood was drawn. Witnesses on each side claimed that the other side had backed down first. Though most accounts blame Tecumseh's impassioned speech for the near fight, one story states that Tecumseh started it by taking his pipe tomahawk out first. As an explanation, the great leader supposedly said, "I just wanted to have a smoke."

When they met again in July 1811, there was, once more, no progress. Harrison insisted on his right to buy Indian lands from local chiefs, and Tecumseh warned him that if he continued, "You and I will have to fight it out." Harrison recognized that he was dealing with a dangerous enemy; Tecumseh, Harrison wrote, was "one of those uncommon geniuses, which spring up occasionally to produce revolutions and overturn the established order of things."

Later that year, Harrison learned that Tecumseh was away trying to rally southern tribes to his cause. In response, Harrison launched an expedition against Tecumseh's village on the Tippecanoe River. Tecumseh's brother, the Prophet (Tenskwatawa), was in charge and engaged Harrison's troops in battle on November 6, 1811. Though the Americans claimed victory, they suffered heavier casualties. Unable to destroy the Americans, the Indians withdrew, and Harrison burned their village. It was a setback to Tecumseh's plans.

When the War of 1812 broke out, Tecumseh allied with the British and successfully defeated the Americans in a series of battles on the Detroit frontier. In the spring of 1813, Tecumseh and Harrison opposed each other once again at the Siege of Fort Meigs. The failure of the British and Indian forces to take Fort Meigs marked a change in the course of the war. That September, the English lost control of the Great Lakes in the Battle of Lake Erie and had to withdraw from the Detroit area. On October 5, Harrison's forces defeated the fleeing British, and Tecumseh was killed at the Battle of the Thames. The physical conflict between Harrison and Tecumseh, which began at Fallen Timbers, ended nineteen years later, though some argue this was just the start of their legend.

Tecumseh's Curse, or the Curse of Tippecanoe

For almost twenty years, the Shawnee leader Tecumseh and William Henry Harrison fought for the future of the Northwest Territory. On October 5, 1813, Tecumseh was killed at the Battle of the Thames by forces under Harrison's command. That was the end of their conflict—or so many thought. Harrison went on to amass a fortune and advance his political career. In 1840, he was elected president of the United States, running on the slogan "Tippecanoe and Tyler Too." He took office on March 4, 1841, fell ill and died exactly a month later on April 4, 1841.

Harrison came into office with great expectations. He was going to restore the Whig party to greatness, and he was going to implement policies to reverse the excesses of the Andrew Jackson era. But none of that happened. It was as if a supernatural force had struck him down at the peak of his power and at the climax of an ambitious career. It looked like he had been cursed.

Tecumseh's brother, the Prophet (Tenskwatawa), was a Shawnee holy man and mystic. Legend has it that he placed a curse on Harrison and any U.S. president elected in a year that ends in 0. Lincoln, Garfield and McKinley were elected in 1860, 1880 and 1900, respectively, and were all assassinated in office. Harding and Franklin Roosevelt were elected in 1920 and 1940, respectively, and both died in office. John Kennedy, elected in 1960, was also assassinated in office.

Some believe that Ronald Reagan, elected in 1980, broke the curse when he was shot in office but survived. Whether eerie coincidence or evidence of supernatural influence, the curse appears to be over. George W. Bush became president in 2000 and survived two terms intact.

Tecumseh's Revenge

William Henry Harrison defeated Tecumseh and blunted his efforts to unify the Native Americans, but it is Tecumseh who is remembered. Harrison has become a historical trivia question, while the story of Tecumseh thrives. Even in his lifetime, Harrison was often a footnote in the story of Tecumseh. Some have called this phenomenon Tecumseh's Revenge.

The Shawnee's charisma and leadership were inspiring. In an era when torture and abuse of wartime prisoners were almost the norm, his mercy and compassion stood out. Not only did Tecumseh speak out against mistreatment of prisoners, but he also acted against this injustice. On a cold, rainy May morning in 1813, in the ruins of Fort Miamis, a group of unruly warriors were amusing themselves by murdering American prisoners. An enraged Tecumseh rode into the group and threatened them with immediate death if another prisoner was harmed. No one present that day ever forgot it. That morning, in what is now Maumee, Ohio, the Shawnee leader put himself between a ragged group of unarmed prisoners and his own warriors. On that day, Tecumseh became more than a great leader and warrior; he became a legend.

Six months later, outnumbered and pursued by Harrison's army, the remains of the English and Native forces made a stand along the Thames River in what is now Ontario. The English General Proctor fled for his life. The remaining British regulars offered token resistance and then surrendered. Tecumseh could have escaped, but he chose to stand and fight with his warriors. And he died with them. The Americans mutilated the Indian bodies so badly that it was impossible to identify which one was Tecumseh's. Though Tecumseh was defeated, his choice to stand with his people and die in a hopeless fight gave his legend wings of fire.

In Harrison's lifetime, towns, places and even people (e.g., William Tecumseh Sherman) were named after his opponent. Books were written, paintings were painted and stories were told and retold. Harrison achieved success, but Tecumseh achieved greatness.

In American culture, Tecumseh represents the noble savage. The problem, though, is that he wasn't a savage. He was smarter, braver and

The gates of Fort Miamis, where an unknown number of Kentucky militiamen were killed on May 5, 1813. *Photo by author.*

more compassionate than his foes. We sympathize with his cause and his dedication, even though he was fighting us. We cannot look at the story of Tecumseh without seeing how we, as a nation, dealt with growth, greed and Native Americans. We cannot look at Tecumseh's greatness and ignore our own shortcomings, and that, precisely, is Tecumseh's revenge.

LITTLE TURTLE AND BLUE JACKET: A PARTNERSHIP TOO GREAT TO LAST

After the Treaty of Greenville was signed, Anthony Wayne wrote a letter to Secretary of War James McHenry describing the chiefs involved. He referred to Blue Jacket as "the famous Shawanoe Chief Blue Jacket, who, it is said, had the Chief command of the Indian Army." He described Little Turtle as one "who also claims that honor & who is his rival for fame and power."[6] Two hundred years later, there are still questions about that rivalry.

Sometime around 1790, Blue Jacket moved his people to the Maumee River close to the Miami village of Kekionga (current-day Fort Wayne, Indiana). Several miles east on the Eel River was the village of Miami war chief Little Turtle. The two combined forces and destroyed every army sent against them. They were so effective, in fact, that by 1793, white immigration into the Ohio Territory had come to a halt.

Traditionally, much of the credit for this effectiveness goes to Little Turtle. Many have proclaimed Little Turtle a brilliant military leader and tactician. William Henry Harrison, who fought at Fallen Timbers and, later, in the War of 1812, once said, "'A safe leader is better than a bold one.' This maxim was a great favorite of Caesar Augustus…who…I believe, [was] inferior as a warrior to Little Turtle."[7]

Following the Treaty of Greenville in 1795, Little Turtle made a great effort to learn white ways and ease tensions between his people and the steadily encroaching whites. Mild mannered and likable, he became a favorite of early white settlers. Additionally, his white son-in-law, William Wells, did much to enhance his reputation among whites.

The argument for Little Turtle being the brains behind the Northwest Indian Confederacy is strong. The Miamis attempted to stay out of the American Revolution until it was forced on them. In 1780, an American army led by a French adventurer named Augustin de La Balme attacked the Miami villages. Little Turtle surrounded La Balme's camp and destroyed him. Little Turtle fans point to this battle as an early indication of his tactical ability. It was impressive and did indeed show that Little Turtle had command and control over his band of Miamis. In 1790 and 1791, Little Turtle and a confederacy of Northwest Indian Tribes used similar tactics to destroy armies under American General Josiah Harmar and Arthur St. Clair. Some historians have gone so far as to name the Indian War of the Old Northwest "Little Turtle's War."

However, historian John Sugden does not agree. In his biography of Blue Jacket, Sugden argues that the Shawnee chief was the leader behind the Indians' success. Blue Jacket was the more experienced of the two. He had fought at the Battle of Point Pleasant in 1774 and, for almost twenty years, was continuously engaged in combat operations against the Americans. His skill and experience made him the most feared Native leader on the frontier.

Both Blue Jacket and Little Turtle were described as tall (over six feet) and physically imposing. Both were highly intelligent war chiefs. Both were interested in white ways. At various times, they both built white-style homes and owned livestock. Both were skilled in business and worked with white traders for personal profit. Both men were friendly and likable yet ruthless and brutal in combat.

Despite these similarities, their personalities were strikingly different. Little Turtle was quiet and unassuming. Blue Jacket was vain and egotistical. Little Turtle never drank liquor. Blue Jacket was fond of good food, good drink and an occasional binge. Their collaboration reached a high point on the morning of November 4, 1791. Blue Jacket and Little Turtle, working with the major chiefs of the Ohio tribes, assembled a Native army and quietly and efficiently encircled a larger United States army of over one thousand men and camp followers. At dawn, the Native army attacked and destroyed the entire U.S. army. It remains one of the greatest defeats ever suffered by an American army.

However, Blue Jacket and Little Turtle's glory was short-lived. By the summer of 1794, divisions in the Native American alliance began to appear. Friction between the tribes led to some questionable decisions and a disastrous attack on Fort Recovery. As Anthony Wayne's army moved north, tensions increased. At a council in early August, Little Turtle spoke against fighting Wayne, saying, "The Americans are now led by a chief who never sleeps. The night and the day are alike to him." Little Turtle urged listening to Wayne's peace offers, but Blue Jacket and the other chiefs overruled him. Little Turtle agreed to lead his Miamis but played no leadership role in the Battle of Fallen Timbers. Blue Jacket gets sole credit for the loss.

In 1795, though, the anti-American Blue Jacket had a change of heart. Having lost faith in the English and seeing no future in resistance, he led his people to Greenville to make peace. Blue Jacket assumed a leadership role in the negotiations with Wayne. Little Turtle apparently resented this; as a result, the Miami chief arrived late to the negotiations and was the last to sign the Treaty of Greenville.

Blue Jacket asked Wayne to arrange a trip to Philadelphia so the chiefs could meet with President Washington. A delegation under Blue Jacket went in 1796, and a delegation under Little Turtle went later. The two chiefs refused to travel together.

The two remained enemies for the remainder of their lives. Little Turtle strove to keep the peace and pushed cooperation between the Miami and the whites. Blue Jacket remained at peace but entertained talk of further resistance and encouraged the young Tecumseh. Blue Jacket died of natural causes in 1810, and Little Turtle followed in 1812. The debate between supporters of Weyapiersenwah and supporters of Mihšihkinaahkwa will probably never be resolved. What is not disputed, though, is that they defeated the United States repeatedly, stunned the world and almost achieved the impossible.

CHAPTER 2

THE INVADERS

The Americans

Augustin de La Balme's Quest for Glory

Glory is fleeting, but obscurity is forever.
—Napoleon Bonaparte

In early 1777, a ship hired by the nineteen-year-old Marquis de Lafayette anchored off the coast of South Carolina. Lafayette and a small group of French adventurers rowed ashore to join the Americans in the fight against England. Among the group was Augustin de La Balme, a French calvary officer and veteran of the Seven Years' War. La Balme had written two books on calvary tactics and considered himself an expert. He expected to lead George Washington's calvary. In the summer of 1777, he fought as a colonel with the Americans but failed to impress Washington. In the fall, Washington appointed Casimir Pulaski general of the American mounted troops. Angry at being passed over, La Balme resigned from the Continental army but stayed in America looking for a way to prove himself.

In 1780, La Balme arrived in the Illinois Territory with a bold plan. Claiming to have secret orders from George Washington, he planned to recruit French settlers and traders in the region to form a militia. He would move up the Wabash River and then down the Maumee River with the goal of capturing British-held Detroit. The American commander, George Rogers Clark, and La Balme did not get along, but Clark saw no reason to stop him. In the beginning, La Balme's campaign did have some success. He was able to raise a small force of over one hundred men and find horses

Detail of Italian American painter Ettore Caser's 1931 mural *The Battle of Fallen Timbers*. *Photo by author.*

for them. As his militia moved through central Indiana, he flew the flag of France and told residents he was on a mission from the king of France.

La Balme, though, made several critical mistakes. He was wrong about the frontier Frenchmen, who lived, worked and intermarried with Native Americans. Few were eager to take sides with either the Americans or the British, and most did not rally to La Balme's cause. Secondly, he grossly underestimated the fighting ability of the Native Americans. He assumed the "savages" would not be a serious problem. Because his mounted men moved quickly, the Indians were unable to organize any resistance at first, and it appeared he was right. La Balme reached the Miami village of Kekionga (modern-day Fort Wayne, Indiana) and sacked the English and French trading posts there. Because it was fall, most of the Miami men were out hunting, so there was no opposition.

La Balme stayed in Kekionga for two weeks, waiting for reinforcements that never came. While they waited, the French militia killed Miami livestock, ate Miami food stores, got drunk on trade store rum and generally behaved badly. La Balme learned of a nearby village on the Eel River with an English

Augustin de La Balme. *Courtesy of the American Battlefield Trust.*

trading post. Leaving a small detachment behind in Kekionga, he set out for the Eel River village. By this point, the Miami were very tired of Colonel de La Balme, and the Miami hunters, led by Chief Pacanne, had returned to Kekionga. The twenty Frenchmen left there were wiped out.

In the early morning hours of November 5, warriors from the Eel River village under the command of a little-known war chief named Mihšihkinaahkwa (Little Turtle) surrounded La Balme's camp. At sunrise, the Miami attacked. The French fired one round before they were overwhelmed and destroyed. There were few survivors. The bodies were left for the wolves. The victory made Little Turtle famous. Years later, he used similar tactics to destroy two American armies.

Little Turtle achieved greatness. Lafayette went on to fight in both the American and French Revolutions and is beloved in both countries. Augustin de La Balme, the man who claimed to have secret orders from George Washington and the king of France, is remembered as a footnote and by a roadside marker on a small country road in Indiana.

Thirty Men Make a Stand: Harmar's Campaign

Some historians believe that the Fallen Timbers campaign represents the birth of the United States Army. The American Revolution was fought by a makeshift army under the jurisdiction of the Continental Congress. When the war ended, the Continental army was disbanded, and only a battery of artillery at West Point and a small regiment on the frontier were left intact.

There was intense debate among the founding fathers over the necessity of a professional army. Many felt that militias could do the job. Militias are inexpensive and locally controlled, while national armies are expensive and federally controlled. Federalists such as Washington and Hamilton felt that a well-trained professional military was the only way to protect the nation.

They argued that local militias were often poorly trained and undisciplined. The Indian Wars proved them right.

After two campaigns with armies composed largely of militia ended with death and defeat, Congress found the money to create and train a professional army under Major General Anthony Wayne. Wayne's campaign, culminating in the Battle of Fallen Timbers, was the first successful operation conducted by the United States Army. From that small battle on the Maumee, the U.S. military grew to be one of the most effective and powerful fighting forces the world has ever known.

Some historians, though, take another approach and maintain that the U.S. military was born in a forgotten swamp almost four years before the Battle of Fallen Timbers. In the fall of 1790, a fighting force of 320 regulars and 1,100 militia left current-day Cincinnati, Ohio, under the command of General Josiah Harmar, on a campaign to punish the allied Native tribes of the Northwestern Confederacy. They traveled north, burning several villages, until they reached the Miami village of Kekionga (modern-day Fort Wayne, Indiana). On October 19, Harmar sent a small detachment of thirty regulars and approximately two hundred militiamen under the command of Colonel John Hardin to investigate an Indian village to the northwest on the Eel River.

Little Turtle and Le Gris of the Miami, Blue Jacket of the Shawnee and Buckongahelas of the Lenape were watching and set a trap. From the beginning, the American militiamen acted badly. Many slipped away to return to camp, and a mounted unit was forgotten after a midday break and left behind. The Americans discovered a trail of discarded Indian gear, leather pieces and pieces of beadwork, and the militia outpaced the regulars in their desire to score some real Indian swag.

But then they came to a meadow. The meadow had a swamp on one side and thick forest on the other two sides. At the far end of the meadow, smoke rose from a dying campfire. Beads and Indian items lay strewn about on the ground. It was obviously a trap. The only thing it lacked was a scantily dressed maiden throwing kisses and calling, "Yoo-hoo, militia boy!" The militia fell for it and rushed into the pocket. The regulars, in a disciplined march, were only halfway across the meadow when the trap was sprung.

The woods behind the bait erupted in a roar of musket fire. Several men, including the son of General Charles Scott, were killed outright. The militia and the regulars moved to the left and were hit with a solid volley from that side. The thirty regulars under the command of Captain John Armstrong formed a line. The militiamen panicked, dropped their weapons and fled. The stampeding militia ran into and over the regulars, breaking their line. Captain Armstrong of the regulars was knocked into the swamp. When he lifted his head from the muck, he witnessed something incredible. Twenty-two regulars and eight militiamen, without officers, had reformed the line and were resisting the Indian advance. They fired one volley, and then the Indians were on them with tomahawks and war clubs. The soldiers fought with bayonets; not one surrendered, not one ran and not one of them survived.

Historian Wiley Sword wrote, "It was perhaps a humble beginning for the modern United States Army, yet a proud combat tradition was rapidly emerging." Late that night, Captain Armstrong stumbled back into Harmar's camp. In tears, he denounced the cowardly militia and told his commander that his men had sold their lives dearly, saying, "They fought and died hard."[8]

Harmar withdrew his main force the next day. Scouts reported that the Natives were back in Kekionga. On October 22, Harmar sent a force of about five hundred men back to surround the village and engage the Native forces. Little Turtle and Blue Jacket were waiting. In the two battles of Kekionga, the Indians outmaneuvered and outfought the Americans. Almost half of the American forces were killed or wounded. Realizing that his regulars were outnumbered, and the terrified militiamen were almost useless, Harmar was forced to retreat to Cincinnati.

Sadly, the exact spot where Armstrong's men made their heroic stand is uncertain. For many years, there was a roadside marker on Carroll Road, northwest of Fort Wayne, which read:

> *Colonel John Hardin, of the Kentucky Militia, with 180 men and Captain John Armstrong, U.S. Army, with 30 men, were routed here on October 19, 1790, by Indians under Miami Chief Little Turtle during General Harmar's Campaign.*

Around 2005, the marker was hit by a vehicle and destroyed. The Indiana authorities reviewed the marker and decided not to replace it because they did not know how many militiamen were actually involved or if this was actually the exact spot. Additionally, there is some debate as to whether Little Turtle was in sole command.[9]

Today, there is nothing official to commemorate the site. However, in a twist that could only have come from Ripley's Believe It or Not!, there is a military presence there, as Riverview Cemetery is on the other side of the road. In that cemetery is a memorial to twentieth-century American war veterans built around a decommissioned U.S. M41 tank. Overlooking the spot where the spirit of the U.S. Army was born in a melee of tomahawks and bayonets is a U.S. army tank designed for close infantry support.

John Hardin: Bold, Courageous and Bloodthirsty

Colonel John Hardin (not to be confused with Old West outlaw John Wesley Hardin) presents a challenge to modern-day historians. He was an uncommonly good marksman with the long rifle. He was brave in combat and a natural leader. In short, he personified the image of the rugged American frontiersman. But he was also impulsive, headstrong and murderous. He called himself the Indian Killer.

Born on the Virginia frontier, Colonel Hardin enlisted in the Virginia militia and, in 1774, fought in Lord Dunmore's War. Hardin was wounded and carried a musket ball in his body for the rest of his life. During the American Revolution, he served as one of Daniel Morgan's riflemen and distinguished himself at the Battle of Saratoga fighting the British.

After the war, he found land in Kentucky and moved his family there in 1786. His pioneer farm was barely established when he joined George Rogers Clark's 1786 Wabash campaign. The campaign resulted in several Indian villages being destroyed and a considerable loss of life among the Native Americans. It was not a military success and is sometimes cited as the beginning of the Northwest Indian War. During the campaign, Hardin led an attack on a friendly Piankeshaw village. In 1789, as a major in the Kentucky militia, Hardin led another raid into Indian land against a Shawnee village. Despite the fact that this raid did more harm than good to the American cause, Hardin returned home a hero with twelve scalps.

Hardin never missed a chance to attack and kill Indians. He was part of Harmar's 1790 expedition and the disaster at Kekionga. The American fight on the Eel River is known as Hardin's Defeat. Attacking headlong with ruthless aggressiveness was his trademark. In March 1791, Hardin and his men were part of an expedition led by General Charles Scott of Kentucky. Scott's son had been killed at Hardin's Defeat, and Scott was an unapologetic Indian hater. He and his men attacked several Wea villages, including Ouiatenon on the Wabash River. They burned the villages and cornfields, killed the men and took forty-one women and children back to Kentucky as prisoners.

In the fall of 1791, Hardin suffered an injury and had to sit out Arthur St. Clair's campaign. St. Clair's catastrophic defeat resulted in the destruction of the U.S. army by Little Turtle and his allies and caused panic on the frontier. St. Clair was relieved of command. With St. Clair out and most of the senior command staff dead or wounded, James Wilkinson rose to the rank of general and took command of Fort Washington (Cincinnati) and several frontier outposts. With his army in tatters and the frontier defenseless, President Washington needed to buy time. He ordered Major Alexander Trueman to go to the Ohio Indian villages and talk peace. Wilkinson decided two messengers would be better than one and sent John Hardin on the peace mission. Wilkinson has earned a place in history as a scheming traitor and a backstabbing villain. The one thing Wilkinson was not, though, was stupid. It is very likely that he knew sending John Hardin, also known as the Indian Killer, on a peace mission was a very bad idea. We don't know if Wilkinson wanted to sabotage the peace talks or if he just wanted to get rid of Hardin. Either way, in May 1792, Hardin and Trueman left Fort Washington on a peace mission. They soon split up, Hardin heading for the upper Maumee and Trueman for the lower Maumee.

Hardin was confident that even if some of the Indians did learn who he was, he would be safe because he carried a letter from George Washington and a wampum peace belt. Hardin traveled with a servant and a translator. They met a "friendly" group of Shawnees who offered to guide them. The Americans at the time (and some historians today) assumed that the friendly Shawnees did not know who Hardin was. There is evidence, however, that by this point in the war, the Shawnees had a well-developed communication and intelligence network. It is likely they knew exactly who Hardin was when they killed him in his sleep. The location of his death is today the town of Hardin in Shelby County, Ohio. Major Trueman and his interpreter were in Lower Tawa Town (Ottawa, Ohio) when they were also killed.[10]

With two armies destroyed and peace messengers dead in the wilderness, the U.S. Congress had no choice but to agree with President Washington's demand for a new standing army and a new commander. After Hardin's death, both sides found themselves on the road to Fallen Timbers.

Hardin's fearlessness in battle and his death while under a white flag made him an early American hero. Towns, counties and schools have been named after him. It was only later that history began to recognize that his failure to follow orders cost American lives in battle. We are also coming to terms with the fact that his attacks on Indian villages resulted in unforgivable horror and the unnecessary deaths of many women and children.

In early American accounts, the death of Hardin is described as a treacherous murder. From the Native American perspective, it was the justifiable execution of a war criminal.

The Heroic Life and Forgotten Death of Colonel Alexander Truman

The study of history can be surprising. Our ability to use the internet to compare research and find sources is changing everything. Sometimes what we find can even shock.

Growing up, I read everything I could find on the local history of my hometown. During the '70s, I read volumes of fresh material published for the bicentennial. After college, I worked on the local newspaper and continued to feed my love of history by researching and writing articles on local history. I learned a great deal about the history of Ottawa, Ohio.

Many years later, living in Maumee, Ohio, I became involved with the efforts to preserve the Fallen Timbers Battlefield. I read everything I could find on the battle. I listened to countless programs by historians, archaeologists and writers. I learned a great deal about the Battle of Fallen Timbers.

In 2023, I was researching a minor player in the story of the Northwest Indian Wars when a tiny footnote jumped out at me. "Colonel Alexander Truman killed in April 1792 on the site of current day Ottawa, Ohio." I was stunned. How was it that in a lifetime of studying frontier and local history, I had never heard of an American war hero who was killed by Indians while on a mission for George Washington in my backyard? The story of Colonel Trueman or Truman is a footnote in frontier history but an excellent example of how sometimes heroes are almost forgotten while other less admirable characters are glorified.

Though there were no popular novels, songs or stories about the life of Alexander Truman, there are records, and records sometimes tell the real story. Many years after his death, Truman's descendants petitioned the government for pension money promised him for service in the American Revolution. According to their documentation, he was born in Maryland in 1750. He joined the Continental army in 1776 and served as a captain in the Sixth and Second Maryland Regiments. He fought throughout the war, seeing action at the battles of Camden and Cowpens, and was present at Yorktown.[11] The Maryland regiments were disbanded at the end of the war.

Truman married and had three children.

From military records, we learn that in 1790, Truman rejoined the U.S. Army.[12] In 1791, he was commanding a company of mounted dragoons under General Arthur St. Clair. The morning of November 3, 1791, St. Clair's army was camped on the Wabash River. During the night, a confederacy of every major Native American tribe in the Northwest surrounded the camp. At dawn, they attacked.

From testimony given during a later inquiry into St. Clair's actions, we learn that Truman was able to get his company of dragoons mounted to resist the Indian attack. At one point in the battle, Truman was ordered to break through the surrounding Native American line. In a saber charge, he broke through the Shawnee line and moved ahead of infantry support. The Shawnee surrounded his company and cut them down. Of the fifty men in Truman's company, all but thirteen were killed. Truman was shot in the left hip and wrist. While a fellow soldier was helping him back to the American line, a bullet cut two fingers off his left hand.[13]

Despite his wounds, Truman was still active. Just before the Americans withdrew, he located a surviving packhorse and helped to hoist the obese and gout-ridden General St. Clair onto the horse's back, probably saving the general's life.[14] St. Clair's Defeat, also known as the Battle of a Thousand Slain, is by some accounts the worst defeat ever suffered by the U.S. military, with a 97 percent casualty rate.

There was an official inquiry. Truman survived his wounds and was sent to Philadelphia to testify. With almost no army to defend the frontier, President Washington decided to attempt a peace treaty. Secretary of War Henry Knox approached Truman and asked him to undertake an extremely dangerous mission. Truman agreed to approach the tribes of the Northwest to ask for a ceasefire. He was given a letter from George Washington and a string of wampum.

Truman returned to Fort Washington, modern-day Cincinnati, and prepared to head north. General James Wilkinson decided two peace envoys would be better than one and recruited Colonel John Hardin for the job. Hardin was also a veteran of the Revolutionary War and was well known on the frontier. He had a reputation as a marksman and a fearless militia leader. He was also impulsive and ruthless. He was proud

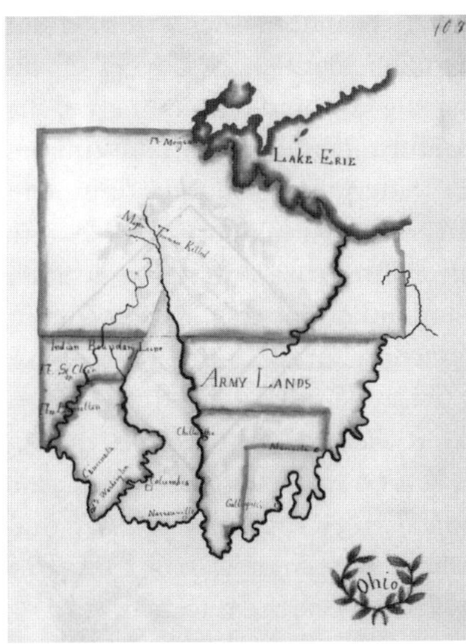

In April 1823, a young girl named Frances Henshaw, put together a "Book of Penmanship" to show off her penmanship and cartography. This beautiful map of Ohio includes a notation: "Major Truman killed." *David Rumsey Map Collection: Frances Henshaw.*

of killing Indians and burning Indian villages. He may have been the worst possible choice for a peace mission. In May 1792, Hardin and Truman started north. They split up, Hardin heading for the Miami villages, around current-day Fort Wayne, Indiana, and Truman aiming for the villages' center at the confluence of the Auglaize and Maumee Rivers (current-day Defiance, Ohio).

A party of Shawnee met Hardin, who was traveling with a servant and an interpreter. Though what happened is sometimes portrayed as a random act of violence, it is almost certain the Shawnees knew who Hardin was and intentionally executed him. Truman and a cook were also intercepted by Indians and killed. They thought Truman was a spy and did not believe the Americans wanted peace. Ironically, part of him did make it to the Maumee. A captured American who knew Truman and his cook was working on a boat on the Maumee for British Indian agent Alexander McKee when, in the spring of 1792, he was shown two scalps, which he identified as belonging to Truman and his cook.

That is generally where history leaves it. Hardin and Truman's failed peace mission is a footnote in the Indian Wars. It served to harden American attitudes toward the Native American resistance and led almost directly to the Battle of Fallen Timbers.

Early written accounts confuse the site of Truman's death. Some say it was on the Ottawa River, also known as Hog Creek, and some say it was in an Ottawa village. It appears that the question was sorted out not by historians but by genealogists. Researchers looking into the Truman family history found evidence indicating that he was killed in an Odawa (Ottawa) village known as Lower Tara Town on the Blanchard River. The website Find a Grave states that he was likely killed on the current site of the Putnam County Courthouse in Ottawa, Ohio.[15]

This came as a shock to me. For six years, early in my career, I worked as a reporter for the *Putnam County Sentinel*, which then was located directly across the street from the courthouse. Every morning, I would park in a lot along the Blanchard River and go to the office, and at some point in the day, I'd cross the street to the courthouse to check on local crime and punishment. The idea that I was retracing the last steps of a Revolutionary War hero with a letter in his pocket signed by George Washington would have seemed ridiculous to me. Sometimes history is literally underfoot.

Anthony Wayne, the Underwhelming Choice

Brave and nothing else.
—Thomas Jefferson on Anthony Wayne

The triumph of the Native American forces over Arthur St. Clair's army in November 1791 left President Washington dealing with a crisis. Among the many issues Washington and his advisors faced was the selection of a commander for the army. Most of the Revolutionary War generals were either too old, had health issues or had been politically or socially compromised. Several had turned to the bottle to battle peacetime boredom, and one had been outed for his fondness for young men, which, in 1792, was a career killer; he was termed "impetuous in his temper."

Anthony Wayne. Pastel by James Sharples Sr., circa 1795, after Fallen Timbers. *United States Army Center of Military History.*

Josiah Harmar was an experienced professional, but the failure of his Kekionga campaign had made him unemployable. Likewise, Arthur St. Clair's incompetence led to his dismissal. The Battle of the Wabash gutted the American officer corps, leaving few officers to promote. Among the losses were Major General Richard Butler, dead; Major Heart, Second Regiment, dead: Lieutenant Colonel Drake, First Levies, badly wounded; Lieutenant Colonel George Gibson, Second Levies, mortally wounded; Major Ferguson, artillery commandant, dead; Captain Alexander Trueman, commander of the calvary, wounded; and Lieutenant Colonel Oldman of the Kentucky Militia, dead.[16]

James Wilkinson was currently in command, but as Jefferson noted, "He has many unapprovable points in his character." Washington and his advisors looked at a list of aging and uninspiring former officers, and only one name survived the cut. General Anthony Wayne got the job almost by default. He drank but was not a drunk. He womanized but avoided serious scandal. He was egotistical and loved comfort but was not corrupt. His war record showed courage but no special talent. He was a stern disciplinarian but (by the standards of the day) not excessively brutal. About Wayne, Washington wrote, "Whether sober—or a little addicted to the bottle, I know not." So, with little enthusiasm, Wayne became Major General Anthony Wayne.

Raised in Pennsylvania, Wayne was a moderately successful farmer before the war. When the revolution began, Wayne joined the military and left his farm (and wife and children) behind. He earned a reputation during the war for discipline, bravery and loyalty. He became famous for taking the British outpost Stoney Point in a nighttime attack using only edged weapons (bayonets and swords). As a civilian, he had failed in business and politics. Broke, unemployed and estranged from his family, he knew the army was his last chance. He might not have been a master of strategy, but he understood discipline and tactics. He turned out to be the right choice for building an army and pounding home the basics. He also had another thing in his favor: he was "Mad Anthony."

The Brilliant Madness of Anthony Wayne

Or How Anthony Wayne Saved the Marquis de Lafayette and Won the American Revolution

Over a million tourists visit the Virginia's historic triangle each year. Colonial Williamsburg, Jamestown and Yorktown are important sites in American history. As the visitors move about from site to site, very few are likely to notice a historic marker on Route 5 just south of Williamsburg. The Green Spring battlefield has no visitors center, only one interpretive sign and no trail. This sadly forgotten battle may have been one of the most important of the American Revolution.

There are several versions of how Anthony Wayne got his nickname Mad Anthony. We know the name was used well before the Battle of Green Spring, but Wayne's actions that day made it permanent. During the spring

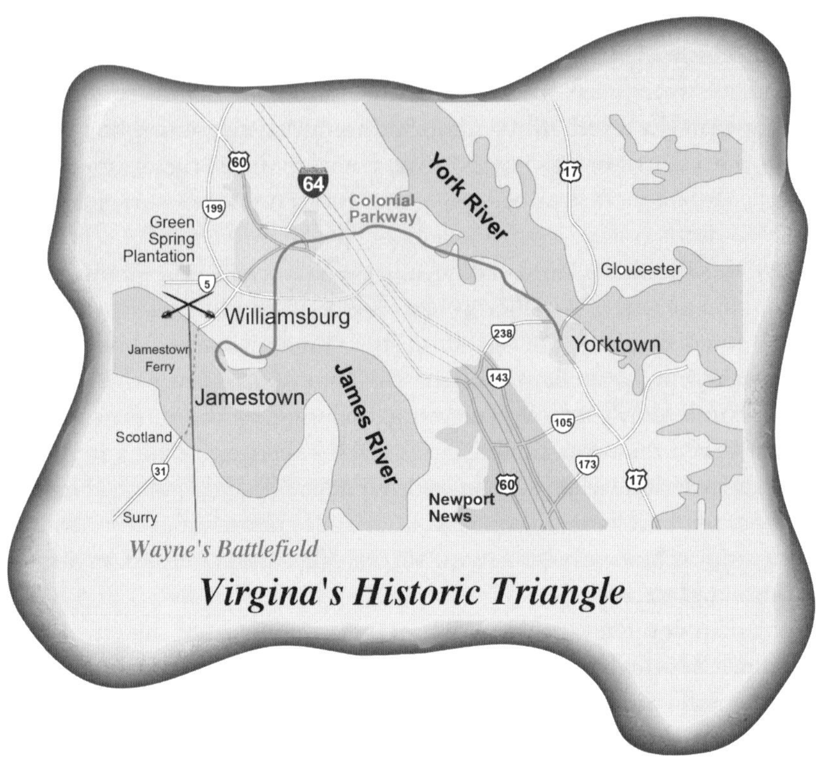

Virginia's Historic Triangle. *Map by author.*

of 1781, the bold young French soldier Lafayette had been harassing the vastly larger English army in Virginia under the command of Lord Cornwallis. Lafayette, despite being only twenty-four years old, had all the Americans in the area under his command, including some Pennsylvanians led by thirty-four-year-old Anthony Wayne. Cornwallis desperately wanted to pin down the elusive American army and capture Lafayette. Lafayette was young, dashing and very popular with the Americans. Capturing him would have had a devastating effect on American morale.

On July 6, 1781, Lafayette saw a chance to cripple Cornwallis. The British were in the process of ferrying their army across the James River. John Graves Simcoe (who would later become governor of Canada) crossed over with the Queen's Rangers. The Americans were fed false intelligence indicating that most of the British army had crossed over, leaving a small force unprotected on the north bank. With about five hundred men,

Anthony Wayne advanced to the crossing, followed by Lafayette's army. Too late, Wayne and Lafayette realized it was a trap. Cornwallis had hidden the bulk of his army in a wooded area on their left. With the James River on their right, the greatly outnumbered Continentals were surrounded on three sides.

In his 2021 biography of Lafayette, *Hero of Two Worlds*, Mike Duncan states that Wayne had two options: "He could cry retreat, most likely triggering a panicked flight and ultimate defeat: or he could stand his ground and fight." Had he stood and fought, Wayne would most likely have been surrounded and quickly destroyed. Wayne chose a third option. He ordered his men to fix bayonets and charge. Stunned and confused, the British halted their attack. The Americans approached, to within fifty yards of the English. Both sides formed firing lines and proceeded to pour volley after deadly volley into each other. The field turned red with blood. The bold move confused the English and gave Lafayette enough time to organize an orderly retreat. As a result, Lafayette and Wayne escaped with their army intact.

Cornwallis withdrew to Yorktown to resupply by sea. Unfortunately for Cornwallis, the French navy cut him off. Washington and French General Comte de Rochambeau brought their armies to Virginia to join Lafayette and Wayne. The French and American forces laid siege to Yorktown. On October 19, 1781, Cornwallis was forced to surrender his entire army. Yorktown is considered the battle that won the war—made possible, perhaps, by "Mad Anthony" Wayne.

Among the American forces that July day were two young officers who were to play a role in Northwest Ohio history. Richard Butler went on to become General Richard Butler and would die on the banks of the Wabash in St. Clair's Defeat. Amos Stoddard served in the War of 1812 and was killed during the siege of Fort Meigs. There is a marker on the site dedicated to him. Wayne was criticized at the time for the rashness of his attack, and the matter is still debated today. But be it brilliant or mad, it worked.

> *Madness—Mad Anthony, by God, I never knew such a piece of work heard of—about eight hundred troops opposed to five or six thousand veterans on their own ground.*
>
> —*Unknown writer,* New Jersey Gazette

General James Wilkinson, the Worst Man on the Frontier

On the morning of August 20, 1794, Anthony Wayne's right flank was the first to make contact with the Native Americans at Fallen Timbers. These troops were led by General James Wilkinson, a man Wayne would later describe as "that worst of all bad men." Wayne was right.

Wilkinson was a liar, a schemer, a traitor and possibly an assassin. He was soap opera, old-time Western movie, pointy mustache villain bad. He was a general who never won a battle or lost a court martial, which is significant because he spent more time in court than in battle.

When the American Revolution broke out, Wilkinson joined the Continental army and rose quickly in the ranks through charm and political skill. He was dishonest to the core yet continued to survive. He served as head of the U.S. Army under four presidents, all of whom probably knew he was corrupt but were not quite sure what to do about it.

Wilkinson's career appears to have been built on a lack of loyalty to anyone and an instinctive understanding of when it was time to change sides. He first served under America's most famous traitor, Benedict Arnold. When Arnold's plot was uncovered, Wilkinson turned on him. Wilkinson was then involved in General Horatio Gates's plot to remove Washington. When that plot backfired, Wilkinson turned on Gates. A court of inquiry removed him from command. He then moved to Kentucky, where he involved himself in politics and the local military. He also became a secret agent of the Spanish crown, working against the United States. Agent 13, as he was known, sent information down the river to the Spanish in New Orleans, and the Spanish sent gold up the river to him.

Wilkinson was furious when Washington appointed Anthony Wayne commander of the army instead of him. He sent anonymous letters to the eastern papers accusing Wayne of drunkenness and incompetence. Wayne did not discover Wilkinson's efforts to undermine him until after the battle. He was working to collect evidence of Wilkinson's misconduct and bring him to justice when he died unexpectedly in 1796.

On Wayne's death, Wilkinson became commander of the army, a position he held at various times under Presidents Washington, Adams, Jefferson and Madison. He was involved with Aaron Burr and the alleged conspiracy to form a separate country in the west. When things got hot, he testified against Burr. We now know that this alleged conspiracy was more Wilkinson's plot than Burr's.

General James Wilkinson, by Charles William Peale. *Independence National Historical Park Collection.*

Wilkinson also got involved in a fight with Meriwether Lewis of Lewis and Clark fame. When Lewis died under mysterious circumstances, unnamed sources said he had mental health problems and his death was probably suicide. Historians now think that most of the unknown sources were Wilkinson.

Though no longer the head of the army during the War of 1812, Wilkinson once again took to the field. Old, drunk and fat, he led two failed campaigns (the Battle of Crysler's Farm and the Battle of Lacolle Mills). He was relieved from active service and cleared by a military inquiry. This was at least his fourth court martial.

Wilkinson spent his last years in Mexico City, plotting to form a personal empire in the west. He died in 1826 and was buried in a small Catholic church cemetery. The church was later torn down, the graves were moved and his bones were lost.

Ironically, in all his treachery and betrayal, the person Wilkinson ultimately betrayed was himself. On the morning of August 20, 1794, he competently moved his men into position, anchoring Wayne's right flank while engaging the enemy. This gave the rest of the army time to get into battle formation and defeat the Native Americans. It was probably his most significant battlefield accomplishment and one of the few honest things he ever did. True to character, though, in his desire to betray Wayne, he belittled the battle as a mere skirmish and a minor affair. His chance to take credit for a real accomplishment had come, and he threw it away out of spite.

William Clark: We All Make Mistakes

William Clark, soldier, explorer and leader, is a hero of the United States. He is also a great example of how even great men can get things horribly wrong. As a twenty-four-year-old, he served as a captain in Anthony Wayne's army. He led a rifle company at the Battle of Fallen Timbers under the command of General Wilkinson. When Clark joined the Virginia militia at nineteen, he began the lifelong habit of keeping a daily journal. His journal gives us a fascinating glimpse into the early workings of the military and shows us how effective Wilkinson's campaign of lies, gossip and slander really was.

Clark bought into Wilkinson's misinformation campaign completely and thought Wayne was corrupt, incompetent and cowardly. It is amusing today to reflect on the fact that Clark's source for this opinion, Wilkinson, was actually the corrupt, cowardly traitor—not Wayne. With two hundred years of documentation, we can now say without any doubt that Wilkinson was guilty of treason and that when it came to Wilkinson, young Clark was very wrong.

Clark fought bravely at Fallen Timbers and left us a splendid account of the battle in his journal. His opinion of Wayne appears to have changed, and Clark remained in the army. While Clark was fighting at Fallen Timbers, Meriwether Lewis was in Pennsylvania with the Virginia militia suppressing the Whiskey Rebellion. After leaving the militia, Lewis joined Wayne's legion in 1795 and was placed under Clark's command. The two men became close friends. In 1803, when President Jefferson asked Lewis to explore the American West, Lewis chose Clark as co-captain. While Lewis and Clark explored the heart of the West, Wilkinson met with Aaron Burr and planned an armed insurrection against the government of the United States.

Lewis and Clark marched into history, Burr was taken into custody and tried for treason and Wilkinson slithered off to cause more problems. Following the Corps of Discovery Expedition, Lewis and Clark worked as government agents in the Louisiana Territory. Clark later became governor of the Missouri Territory.

William Clark, by Charles William Peale (1807). *Independence National Historical Park Collection (Philadelphia, Pennsylvania).*

On October 11, 1809, Meriwether Lewis died of two bullet wounds and a stabbing. He had left the frontier and was on his way to Washington. At the time, his death was ruled a suicide, but the Lewis family never accepted the suicide story. Clark was deeply upset by Lewis's death but never questioned it. The Lewis family and a growing number of historians now believe that Lewis was murdered. It may have been a simple robbery or a frontier crime, but evidence of a cover-up suggests something more. Lewis had been having trouble with Wilkinson, who was still in the military and working with the Spanish. It is possible that Lewis headed east with evidence of Wilkinson's crimes, much as Anthony Wayne had done thirteen years earlier, and like Wayne, he never made it. It is also possible that Clark's early support of Wilkinson came back to haunt him in a terrible way.

From the journal of Captain William Clark (his spelling and grammar):

> *20th August 94—A sower of Rain prevented our move at the houre appointed, but we took up the Line of March at 7 o'Clock and found the way extremely bad, much embarrassed by the thickness of the woods on the left and by a number of Steep Reviens on the Right, after proceeding about 2 hours our Spies & advance guard Discovered the Enemy and received their fire, but with inconsiderable Loss were driven back and joined the main Body of the Army, by this time the Right division, Comded by Genl. Wilkinson felt the effects of the Enemeys fire, they was immediately formed & returned the fire, at this period Capt. Campbell troop (Dragoons) made a charge in which he fell & his Troop immediately proceeded through surported by the Infantry's charge which oblidged the enemey to quit theire position and look for more advantagous ground. On our Left & they made an exertion to gaine that Flank but Colo Hamtramck who commanded in that Quarter was perpared & gave them so warm a reception as made theire Situation here as disagreeable as that on the Right, and the charge both on the Right & left both became Genl. & the Enemy was repulsed with precipation;*
>
> *The charge of the Cavelry closed the seene in front & drove the Enemey 3/4 of a mile at the same instant, The Riflemen & Light Infantry, receved a most heavy fire, on the extreem left flank, The Entrepid Lieut. Towls fell at this fire, We drove the Enemy for about one mile directly out, with the Loss of Lieut. Towls & a fiew Infantry on our Side, in this quater was Killed 3 white men & several Indians mostly by the Riflemen. the Troops were now refreshed with ½ a gill of Whiskey which they much required as the action continued more then an houre, the greater part of which time they were in full Speed pressing the Enemey—after remaining on this ground a fiew hours Dureing which time the wounded were Brought in Dressed &c we proceeded within about one mile of the British Garrison and there took up our Encampment.*

GENERAL CHARLES SCOTT, KENTUCKY WARHORSE

Charles Scott, by Paul Sawyer. *Kentucky Historical Society.*

General Charles Scott was commander of the militia at the Battle of Fallen Timbers. He went on to become governor of Kentucky. While he was governor, his political enemies complained that he drank and used profanity excessively. Given the violent and difficult life he led, it would have been more surprising if he didn't drink and cuss.

At the age of seventeen, Scott was orphaned. A local magistrate assigned him to a guardian in a work-for-room-and-board arrangement. Instead, Scott joined the Virginia Regiment and went to fight in the French and Indian War under young Colonel George Washington. He was with General Edward Braddock at the bloody Battle of the Monongahela and served the rest of the war as a scout.

Scott went on to serve under Washington throughout the Revolutionary War. He survived the winter at Valley Forge. In later campaigns, Scott served as Washington's chief of intelligence. Following the war, Scott settled in Kentucky. With James Wilkinson, he helped form the Kentucky Militia. In 1782, Scott's son Samuel was killed, presumably by Indians. Scott lost a second son in Harmar's ill-fated 1790 expedition against the Northwest Tribes. Scott was quick to retaliate.

The Wea, a Miami-speaking people, had several villages on the Wabash River. The principal village, Ouiatenon, was located on a large, fertile prairie, with several smaller villages nearby. On March 9, 1791, Scott's mounted militia swept into the area and destroyed everything. The men were killed, the villages and several hundred acres of cornfields were burned and the surviving women and children were taken prisoner. The village was never rebuilt. Over one hundred captured Indian women and children were held in a hastily erected prison at Fort Washington (present-day Cincinnati). The women and children were imprisoned there for more than a year, in primitive, overcrowded, unsanitary conditions.[17]

During the Fallen Timbers campaign, Scott led the 1,500-man militia force. He is credited with giving Fort Defiance its name, from his comment, "I defy the English, Indians, and all the devils in hell to take it." Wayne was not a believer in the militia system and was critical of militia troops in general, but he respected Scott. Growing mistrustful of his second-in-command, James Wilkinson, Wayne issued a secret order. If he fell in battle or was too severely wounded to lead, command of the entire army, regulars and militia, was to go to Scott.

The tough old soldier also proved to be popular and was easily elected governor of Kentucky in 1808. During his first year in office, Scott slipped on ice on the capitol steps in Georgetown and severely injured his leg. He was forced to walk on crutches the remainder of his life. He urged restraint in the lead-up to the War of 1812, but once war was declared, he supported the effort. In the summer of 1812, he greeted two regiments of Kentucky troops at the governor's mansion. At one point, he was seen banging his crutch against the side of the house and muttering, "If it hadn't been for you, I could have gone with the boys myself."

In August, news that General Hull had surrendered the American army at Detroit reached Kentucky. With the fall of Detroit and several frontier posts, the nation faced disaster. In his last act as governor, Scott commanded a couple of young men to carry him up the steps of the Kentucky capitol so he could sign an order making fellow Fallen Timbers veteran William Henry Harrison the brevet major general over of the Kentucky militia. The order was probably illegal, as Harrison actually lived in Indiana, but Scott had faith in him nonetheless.

The aged and ill Scott retired to his home. After having risked his own life and losing two sons, Scott suffered another loss. In January 1813, his son-in-law Captain Nathaniel G.S. Hart was killed in action at the River Raisin.

At this low point, Scott's choice of Harrison began to pay off. The British and Native American forces were stopped at Fort Meigs. Perry defeated the British navy on Lake Erie, allowing the Americans to recapture Detroit and drive into Canada. On October 5, Harrison crushed English and Native American forces at the Battle of the Thames, and the great Tecumseh fell in battle. The Indian threat was over. Scott died seventeen days later at the age of seventy-four. His lifelong crusade to crush Native American resistance east of the Mississippi had been accomplished.

Solomon Van Rensselaer

Young, Wealthy and Well Connected: Bullets Don't Care

Few military images capture the romantic imagination quite like the cavalry charge. Thundering hooves and flashing sabers are memorable but not always effective. In 1794, mounted troops were called dragoons. They wore gleaming knee-high boots, leather helmets and elaborate uniforms and fought with swords. In some ways, they were the glamour kids of the military.

Solomon Van Rensselaer looked the part. He was born in August 1774 in New York State into the wealthy and politically powerful Van Rensselaer family. His father was a general in American Revolution; he bought Solomon a captain's rank in Anthony Wayne's dragoons.

The heavily wooded Fallen Timbers battlefield was a terrible place for a calvary charge. Captain Mis Campbell attempted to charge into the Indian center and was killed along with several of his men. Twenty-year-old Captain Van Rensselaer was on the Americans' left, which is where the Canadians and Wyandots threatened to turn the line. Leading a charge into timber, Van Rensselaer was a dramatic figure. As he cut down a warrior with his saber, he was shot square in the breastbone. The ball pierced his lung and exited his left shoulder. An American officer recalled seeing him "with the blood rushing from his chest, mouth, and nose." The eyewitness claimed that Van Rensselaer refused treatment and stayed in the saddle until the Indians were on the run.

Solomon Van Rensselaer, by Robert Field, 1797. *Courtesy of Albany Institute of History and Art.*

His annoying upper-class pride probably saved his life. After the battle, a stretcher was built to carry him back to Fort Deposit. He refused to be carried and insisted on riding. "I am an officer of the Cavalry and shall go on horseback."[18] A soldier rode on either side of him to hold him upright. It is believed that the upright position prevented blood from congealing in his lungs, while his spitting and coughing flushed the wound and prevented infection.

Amazingly, Van Rensselaer survived his wounds. His charge made a good (but short) war story. Many a successful political career has been built on far less, but Solomon was not content to rest on his hero status. The privileged young man seems to have developed a talent for charging into situations and getting himself injured. He stayed in the army until 1800, when Jefferson was elected president. Van Rensselaer was an outspoken Federalist. Coincidence or not, many young men who could not separate their Federalist politics from their military service found themselves mustered out under anti-Federalist Jefferson.

In January 1797, Solomon married his first cousin, Harriet Van Rensselaer. From there, he became active in New York State politics. One day, as he was walking along the street in Albany, he attacked opposition politician Elisha Jenkins. Solomon walked up behind Jenkins and began beating him with his cane. It was an unprovoked attack. Sixty-five-year-old John Taylor, a friend of Jenkins, heard of the assault and went looking for Solomon. Taylor and outraged bystanders found Van Rensselaer and beat him almost to death. Van Rensselaer was bedridden for two months. When he recovered, his lawyers threatened legal action against everyone involved in the fight, which Van Rensselaer himself had started.[19]

The Van Rensselaer family's political connections continued to guide Solomon's life. When the War of 1812 broke out, Solomon's cousin Stephen was appointed a general in the New York Militia. Unfortunately, Stephen had no military experience at all, so he appointed Solomon a lieutenant colonel to advise him. In this role, Solomon once again proved to have an exceptional talent for stopping bullets.

The Americans decided to attack Canada across the Niagara River. The Battle of Queenstown Heights was one of the most inept, poorly managed, incompetent and embarrassing actions in the history of the U.S. military. After several delays, infighting among the U.S. officers and near battles between the regulars and the militia, the assault was launched on October 13, 1812. The British saw the Americans rowing across the river and were able to organize an effective defense.

According to Canadian historian Pierre Berton,

> *Colonel Van Rensselaer was hit in the thigh by a musket ball as soon as he stepped out of his boat on the Canadian shore. As he tried to form up his troops, he was promptly hit five more times in the heel, thighs and calf, and though he survived, he spent most of the battle out of action, weak from loss of blood.*

The battle was a decisive victory for the British but may have come at too great a cost. Commanding the English forces was General Isaac Brock. Brock is considered one the best leaders of the war, but he made a fatal mistake that day. Even though the American assault was failing, Brock took a page out of the Van Rensselaer playbook and personally led a charge. He was six foot, four inches tall and dressed in a bright red general's uniform, complete with a plumed hat, a sash and silver and brass trim. The Americans couldn't miss. Brock was killed, and the English war effort never recovered.

Solomon recovered from his wounds and went on to serve briefly as a congressman from New York. He resigned his seat in Congress to take a political appointment. The human bullet sponge died in April 1852 at the age of seventy-eight.

Zebulon Pike: Greatness, Almost

Lieutenant Zebulon Pike, by Benjamin F. Gue. *From* History of Iowa *(1903)*.

Zebulon Pike fought at the Battle of Fallen Timbers—almost. He was on the campaign as a fifteen-year-old, serving under the watchful eye of his father, Zebulon Pike Sr. Zeb Sr. was charged with the defense of Fort Deposit, near present-day Waterville, Ohio. He was a veteran of the Revolution and a trusted professional, which is why the supplies and stores of Wayne's army were guarded by his command. So while Zeb Jr. was with the army, he served a minor role and was not present at the actual battle.

Zebulon Pike discovered the source of the Mississippi River—almost. In 1805, he led an expedition to map and chart the Mississippi River. He made it as far north as Leech Lake, which he believed was the source of the Mississippi. While his mapping and contacts with Native people proved invaluable, he was one lake short of Lake Itasca, which is the real source of the Mississippi.

Lieutenant Zebulon Pike discovered and climbed Pikes Peak—almost. He saw it, but Pike and the men in his party were too malnourished and weak to climb the mountain.

Captain Zebulon Pike led the greatest expedition of exploration in American history—almost. As a captain in the young U.S. Army, he was sent to explore the southern portion of the Louisiana Purchase. Pike and his expedition mapped and explored the U.S. Southwest and made great discoveries. Unfortunately, they wandered into disputed territory and were captured and held as prisoners by the Spanish in Santa Fe. Eventually, Pike was released and returned to the United States. Though his expedition was remarkable and added much to our knowledge of the West, it was overshadowed by the success of the northern expedition led by Lewis and Clark.

General Zebulon Pike won the War of 1812—almost. Promoted to general, Pike led the attack on Fort York, now the city of Toronto. The assault was successful, and the fort fell. A victory of this magnitude might have advanced Pike ahead of several mediocre American generals and changed the course of the war, but this was not to be. Pike and some of his men were resting and enjoying their success when a fuse set by retreating British soldiers ignited the powder magazine, blowing it sky-high. Part of the magazine fell on Pike, killing him instantly.

Pike was an intelligent, loyal and talented soldier, but fate and luck conspired to keep him forever in second place.

Major John Whistler: An American Story

John Whistler ran away from his Northern Ireland home as a young boy and joined the British army. He served in the American Revolution under English General Burgoyne and fought at the Battle of Saratoga. While stationed back in England, Whistler met Anna Bishop and fell in love. The girl's father had a title and did not approve of his well-off English daughter marrying an Irish sergeant in an infantry regiment. The couple eloped and fled to the United States. There, Whistler found that the only job he knew was soldiering. He joined the small, newly formed U.S. Army, and the young couple soon found themselves on the frontier.

Whistler fought in every battle of the Northwest Indian War. He was badly wounded at St. Clair's Defeat (the Battle of the Wabash), but he survived and saw action at Fallen Timbers. In 1795, he helped build Fort Wayne. In 1803, Captain Whistler built Fort Dearborn on the future site of Chicago. He was in command of the fort until 1810. He served during the War of 1812, rising to the rank of major, and was wounded again. When

Arrangement in Grey and Black No. 1, by James McNeil Whistler, 1871. *Courtesy of Musée d'Orsay, Paris.*

the war ended, he helped redesign Fort Wayne before being appointed military storekeeper, a position he held until his death.

John and Anna Whistler had fifteen children. Three of his sons and three of his grandsons were admitted to the West Point Military Academy. Two of his grandsons fought on the Union side in the Civil War. A third served as a surgeon in the Confederate army. John's grandson James, for reasons uncertain, was kicked out of West Point and did not serve. Instead, James went on to pursue a career as an artist, becoming one of the most famous and influential American painters of all time.

The future daughter-in-law of a young Irish lieutenant in Wayne's legion is better known to us as *Whistler's Mother*.

The Wild William May: Sublime Scoundrel

On October 23, 1791, General Arthur St. Clair ordered the execution of three of his soldiers. Two deserters and a man who shot a comrade were hanged in front of the entire army. A fourth man was also accused of desertion, but he pleaded guilty and managed to talk his way out of the noose. The confessed deserter was sent back to his unit. It was not the first time or the last time that William May would be condemned to death and escape through fast talk and luck.

William May, not to be confused with William Wells, was a character straight out of an adventure novel. He was described as a daredevil and a man who thrived on action. He was also violent and possessed of a flexible morality. General James Wilkinson, who has gone down in history as a scoundrel and a traitor himself, described May as "one of the most sublime scoundrels in the Army" but a man "of desperate courage."

A week and a half after hanging the deserters, St. Clair led his army into the disastrous Battle of the Wabash. Over six hundred soldiers were killed and most of the survivors wounded. Among the survivors was Private William May of the First U.S. Regiment. St. Clair was relieved of command, and General James Wilkinson took command of the frontier army in Cincinnati. In April 1792, Colonels John Hardin and Alexander Truman left Fort Washington in Cincinnati on two separate peace missions. When neither was heard from again, Wilkinson came up with a plan. William May had lived with the Indians and spoke enough Algonquian to communicate with most area tribes. Wilkinson sent him to find out what happened to the Hardin and Truman missions. If he ran into unfriendly Indians, the confessed deserter was to pose as a deserter.

May found the bodies of Truman and his cook but was captured by group of Ojibwas. They did not buy his deserter story and proceeded to beat him senseless. Then, once more, May was sentenced to death. Simon Girty, the infamous British Indian agent, intervened and ransomed May before he could be killed. While Girty was taking him as a prisoner to Detroit, May convinced him that in addition to being a frontiersman, a soldier, a deserter and a friend to the Indians, he was a sailor. May was born in Delaware and did know how to handle a boat. Girty turned him over to Alexander McKee, who had a schooner running trade goods and supplies from Canada to McKee's post on the Maumee River. May spent the summer sailing Lake Erie and earning the trust of the Indians and the English.

In September 1792, May's ship was in Niagara, and he saw an opportunity to escape. He arrived in Pittsburgh with detailed knowledge of the British and Native Americans forces. The newly appointed Major General Anthony Wayne was delighted. He referred to May as "a very knowing [and] intelligent person."[19] Wayne rewarded him with $200 and a promotion to sergeant of dragoons. Wilkinson asked Wayne if he might send a letter to the governor of Delaware and ask for a pardon on May's behalf. It seems that May had committed a crime in Delaware and been sentenced to death but escaped from prison.

We don't know if May ever got a pardon, but he was quickly sent back to Cincinnati. Wilkinson kept May and a man named Henry Schaffer in the army, drawing pay and rations, even though they had no military duties whatsoever. Wilkinson believed they might be useful in the upcoming campaign. In the meantime, they got into trouble. On January 6, 1793, May and Schaffer were arrested for "engaging in riotous disorderly conduct," firing their rifles and imitating Indian war cries, "creating false alarms and terrors to the people."[20] They apparently got drunk and shot up Cincinnati. May and Schaffer probably thought this was hilarious, but the three hundred people living in Cincinnati were not amused.

When Anthony Wayne arrived in town with his army, they found work for May and Schaffer. The two joined a group of scouts under the leadership of William Wells. As Wayne began his drive north in the fall of 1793, the scouts were active. Wells was a white man who had been captured by the Miami when he was young and adopted into the tribe. He fought as a warrior at the Battle of the Wabash and then had a change of heart and went over to the American side. In December 1793, Wayne sent a detachment to the site of St. Clair's defeat and built Fort Recovery. St. Clair had left several cannons on the field. The Indians had hidden them. May knew where they were and helped the Americans recover them and mount them in the fort. In the spring and early summer of 1794, the Indian forces harassed American supply lines and launched an attack on Fort Recovery. May saw action and won admiration for his bravery. Wilkinson, who was bitter about Wayne getting the command instead of himself, was critical of almost everyone and everything connected with the campaign except May. May, he wrote, was "a fellow of great activity & resource, of dauntless spirit and violent Passions."

Wells and May dressed and painted themselves like Indians when scouting. They were usually mounted on horses and often far from the main army. In August, Wayne built Fort Defiance and sent Wells and his scouts (or spies, as they were called) toward Roche de Boeuf and Fort Miamis. One night, the spies were returning to Defiance with a couple of prisoners when they passed through an Indian camp. Someone realized who they were, and a sharp firefight broke out. May was in the thick of it. Wells was wounded.

Captain Ephraim Kibby now took command of the scouts. Wayne also had Choctaw and Chickasaw scouts with him. After taking some losses, the Indians decided not to go any farther than Fort Defiance. This put more responsibility on Kibby and his men. On August 18, Wayne stopped at Roche De Beef near current-day Waterville, Ohio. Kibby and his scouts were in the Maumee area when they were discovered by a large group of Indians and had to run for it. May's luck ran out. Racing through a shallow spot in the Maumee River, his horse slipped on the wet rocks and fell. May was captured.

On the evening of August 18, a white captive living with the Indians witnessed May talking to one of his captors. May seemed to think he would talk his way out of it again, but this was not to be. The Indian told him, in effect, "You have lived with us and chose not to stay. You know our language; we can't let you go." William May was out of luck.

On August 19, May was tied to a large burr oak tree on the banks of the Maumee near Fort Miamis. A mark was put on his chest. A group of warriors gathered with rifles and muskets to see who the best marksman was. The next day, the Battle of Fallen Timbers was fought. The following day, the Kentucky militia found May still tied to the tree with at least fifty bullets in him.

It is an unintended irony that the first of many entities to condemn May to death was the State of Delaware and the people who, many years later, did execute him were the Lenape, also known as the Delaware.

THE CURIOUS DEATH OF ANTHONY WAYNE

If a tree don't fall on me, I'll live till I die.
—"Rye Whiskey," by Tex Ritter

In the case of Mad Anthony Wayne, a tree did fall on him, but he still lived until he died two years later, unexpectedly, on December 15, 1796. He had fallen ill after leaving Detroit on a ship and was put ashore at a frontier outpost in current-day Erie, Pennsylvania. His pain was thought to be linked to his gout. After several weeks of suffering, he died. His cause of death was listed as gout of the stomach. In 1809, his son, Colonel

Isaac Wayne, came to Erie to remove his body and rebury him near his family home. When the body was exhumed, Wayne was found to be in an excellent state of preservation, except for his left leg. While the body was almost perfect, the left leg was black and rotted to the point that it almost appeared to be missing.

Wayne's left leg was the one he had complained most about being gouty. It was also the leg he had injured in the summer of 1794. On the afternoon of August 2, Wayne's army made camp on St. Marys River in western Ohio. Wayne had retired to his tent to rest when a tree came crashing down on him. Though he was bruised and shaken, the only damage was to his left leg. It has been speculated that the damaged, gouty left leg led to his death two years later. There is also speculation about how a tree happened to fall on his tent on a windless afternoon.

It may have been foul play. General James Wilkinson, Wayne's second-in-command, was a schemer, a traitor and maybe an assassin. In 1794, he was working as a secret agent of the Spanish government. Fearing that Wayne was going to discover him would have been a solid motive for Wilkinson to attempt murder. Wilkinson was also known to be greedy, ambitious and jealous. The odds of a tree falling on a still day in an army camp and hitting only a general are amazing. To that end, though there is no proof, it is possible that Wilkinson caused the injury that eventually led to Wayne's death.

Two years later, in 1796, Wayne was well aware that Wilkinson was working against him and involved in treasonous activities. Wayne was gathering evidence and testimony against Wilkinson, who he said was "as devoid of principle as he is of honor or fortune." Believing he had enough proof of treason to see Wilkinson hanged, Wayne left Detroit in November to present his case to the authorities. As soon as his ship left Detroit, Wayne fell ill. He was so sick that he was put ashore at a frontier outpost in what is today Erie, Pennsylvania. He lingered for several weeks and then died. The evidence against Wilkinson seems to have disappeared.

A replica of the blockhouse in Erie, Pennsylvania, where Anthony Wayne died. *Postcard in the author's collection.*

Many historians, including Hugh Harrington, editor emeritus of *Journal of the American Revolution*, believe Wayne was poisoned. Harrington points out that before his military career, Wilkinson had been a doctor, and he was familiar with the medicines and poisons of the day. Harrington believes it is very possible that Wilkinson planted someone near Wayne in Detroit to administer the poison and to follow Wayne to Erie. In addition to gout, Wayne had other minor ailments, including stomach and bowel problems, so he would have readily accepted medicine from someone he trusted. Wayne's lingering illness and death in Erie mimic the effects of arsenic poisoning. Harrington argues that Wayne's strange death at exactly this point in time was too beneficial to Wilkinson to be natural.

We cannot know for sure, but the odds of Wayne's death being natural are almost as long as the odds of a tree falling on his tent. In a way, Wayne may have told us he was murdered. When he died, he was quickly buried and not embalmed. When his body was exhumed, many years later, it was almost perfectly preserved. Arsenic kills bacteria and often leaves corpses amazingly intact.

CHAPTER 3

THE CHICAGO CONNECTION

How a Group of Fallen Timbers Survivors Made Windy City History

The Many Lives of Eleanor Lytle McKillip Kinzie

Though few people know it, the Girl Scouts of America have a direct link to the Battle of Fallen Timbers and the incredible life of Eleanor Lytle McKillip Kinzie (1769–1834).

On the morning of August 20, 1794, the battle reached a climax somewhere just south of present-day Monclova Road. Anthony Wayne's regulars pushed into the right flank of the Native American line and ran into a group of Canadian Rangers fighting with the Wyandot and the Ottawas. Heavy fire from the regulars and the Kentucky militiamen poured into the Native line, taking a savage toll on the defenders. One of the dead was Canadian Ranger Captain Daniel McKillip.

McKillip left behind a widow, barely out of her teens, and an infant daughter. Eleanor McKillip was already familiar with war and loss. At the age of nine, while living near Pittsburgh, Eleanor Lytle was taken by a Seneca war party and adopted into the family of the famous Chief Cornplanter (Gyantwachia). According to Eleanor, the chief adored her and gave her the name Gron-we-na, which means "little ship under full sail." After four years of keeping Eleanor in captivity, Cornplanter learned that her parents were still searching for her and, in an act of compassion, returned her to her family, now living in Detroit. In Detroit, as a teenager, Eleanor met Daniel McKillip, and they were married.

Kinzie Mansion and Fort Dearborn. *From Benson Lossing's* Pictorial Field-book of the War of 1812.

When Daniel died at Fallen Timbers, Eleanor faced an uncertain future. Then she met John Kinzie. John was a fur trader and silversmith. He had a trading post near Defiance, which he had to abandon when Wayne's troops occupied the place.

Eleanor and John married in 1798 and moved farther west to live on the shores of Lake Michigan. They are considered the white founders of Chicago and their daughter Ellen is believed to have been the first white child born in what was to become Chicago. Eleanor had four children with John. During the War of 1812, Fort Dearborn was abandoned and its American garrison almost entirely wiped out by Native American forces. Thanks to their Indian friends, the Kinzies survived the battle but not without a series of close calls and adventures. After the war, John Kinzie continued to build a successful business empire. There are still a Kinzie Avenue and a Kinzie Hotel in downtown Chicago.

Eleanor and John's son John Jr. married a bright, educated woman named Juliette Augusta Magill. In 1856, Juliette published a book containing her stories of frontier life and her mother-in-law's many adventures. It is called *Wau-Bun* (*Morning Light*).[21] It was a huge success, becoming one the bestsellers of the age.

When the Kinzies became popular American icons, the death of Eleanor's first husband became a problem. McKillip had died leading men in combat against the United States Army. Because that was a bit of a public relations problem, Daniel's fate got glossed over. Allan Eckert, author of *The Frontiersmen: A Narrative* and the outdoor drama *Tecumseh!*, wrote in his book *Gateway to Empire* that Daniel was accidentally shot by a nervous sentry as he approached Fort Miamis one night. As of this writing, the Wikipedia entry on Daniel states that he was killed by friendly fire at Fort Defiance. Both accounts are based on misinformation that was likely created to please nineteenth-century American readers.

Juliette Gordon Low, great-granddaughter of Eleanor Kinzie, by Edward Hughes, 1887. *Copyright: National Portrait Gallery/Smithsonian.*

Daniel's death at Fallen Timbers was a major event in Eleanor's life and one of the many stories she told to her children and grandchildren. Eleanor's stories of adventure and survival were an influence on the life of John Jr. and Juliette's granddaughter Juliette Gordon Low. Believing that all girls should be as strong and self-sufficient as her great-grandmother Eleanor, Juliette Gordon Low created the Girl Scouts of America. Despite her life of hardship and tragedy, the legacy of the child known as "little ship under full sail" endures.

Margaret McKillip Helm, "Young and Amiable Victim of Misfortune"

Margaret McKillip Helm is both a pioneer heroine and a subject of modern-day controversy. Life on the frontier consisted of shifting alliances, a constantly changing political environment and violence. Margaret was a product of the frontier, a real-life woman who became a legend, a symbol and a subject of controversy.

She was born in Detroit in 1794. Her father was Captain Daniel McKillip, a British soldier. Her mother was Eleanor Lytle McKillip. On the morning of August 20, 1794, Captain McKillip was dressed as an Indian and fighting as a volunteer at Fallen Timbers. His position was on the north side of the battlefield near current-day Monclova Road. He was killed in action.

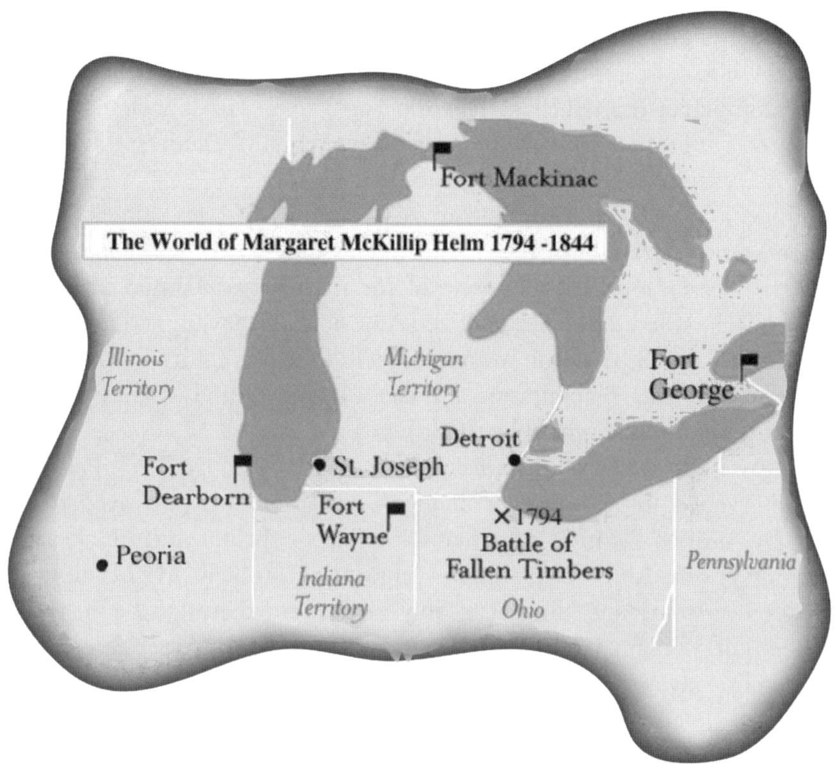

The world of Margaret McKillip Helm. *Map by author.*

In Detroit, his widow, Eleanor, met Indian trader John Kinzie, who had fled Wayne's army. On January 23, 1798, they were married, and Kinzie raised Margaret as his own. The Kinzies moved to what would later become Chicago, where they had four more children and ran a trading post. In 1803, the United States Army built Fort Dearborn near the Kinzie home. At some point, the lovely teenage Margaret caught the eye of a young officer at the fort. By 1812, Margaret, the daughter of an English officer, was married to Lieutenant Linai Helm of the U.S. Army.

When the War of 1812 broke out, the frontier outpost was suddenly vulnerable. General Hull, the American commander in Detroit, ordered Fort Dearborn abandoned. Despite being surrounded by Potawatomi Indians, many of whom favored the British, the post commander, Captain Heald, decided to comply with Hull's orders and march to Fort Wayne. On August 15, 1812, the garrison marched out. On the American side, there was a group of Miami warriors led by Fallen Timbers veteran William Wells, fifty-four U.S. regulars, twelve militiamen, nine women and eighteen children. On the other side were more than five hundred Native Americans, including a Potawatomi chief named Black Partridge, also a veteran of Fallen Timbers. Margaret was in the rear with the wagons, women and children. Lieutenant Helm marched ahead with the regulars.

A mile and a half from the fort, the Americans were attacked. The soldiers were separated from the militia and civilians. Within fifteen minutes, Wells, twenty-six regulars, all twelve of the militia, two women and twelve children were killed. Less than half the Americans survived, and many were wounded. The deaths of the women and children were horrific. According to the Potawatomi, the children were killed by one brutal warrior who was later ostracized and shunned by the tribe.

Margaret and some of the survivors were protected by Black Partridge, who intervened to stop further killing. The Americans portrayed it as a massacre, and the Native Americans saw it as a brutal and quick battle, which they won. All accounts of the battle have problems. Other than the number of Americans killed, the only agreement seems to be regarding the death of William Wells. Both Americans and Native Americans said he behaved bravely and died fighting.

Margaret, who was seventeen years old at the time, survived. Her husband was wounded but alive. They were taken captive by the Indians, who separated them. Margaret was taken to St. Joseph (Michigan) and then to Detroit. Lieutenant Helm was taken first to the Indian villages of Au Sable and then to Peoria before being ransomed and reunited with Margaret in British-held Detroit. The couple then had to travel across lower Ontario in the dead of winter to Fort George on the Niagara River before the English allowed them to return to the United States. Margaret charmed many who met her. A Detroit judge named Woodward, writing to English Colonel Procter on behalf of the Helms, described her as "a young and amiable victim of misfortune." After the war, the Helms returned to Chicago, and they stayed together until 1829, when Margaret divorced her husband for drunkenness and infidelity. She took custody of their son and married Dr. Lucious Abbott in 1836. In 1844, at the age of forty-nine or fifty, she died.

A respected member of her community and a pioneer, Margaret might have gone down as a footnote in history, except fate had other ideas. After death, she achieved national fame, and her story became larger than life.

William Wells, Man of Two Worlds

The morning of August 15, 1812, was hot and steamy along the shores of Lake Michigan. In what is today the city of Chicago, William Wells, a former Indian scout, former American soldier, former Miami warrior and former Indian agent, arose and dressed. He carefully put on his blue U.S. Army officer's uniform, fastened the polished brass buttons, adjusted his sash and then painted his face black. Among the Miami, black paint signifies that a warrior is going into battle prepared to die. That morning, Wells did, in fact, die in battle, just as he predicted. The Battle of Fort Dearborn was a tragic affair fought in sand dunes, and it's still mired in controversy. One fact on which all accounts agree: on that day, Wells conducted himself with honor and died bravely. It was a heroic end to a controversial life.

Wells was born in 1770 to white parents. At the age of sixteen, he was captured by the Miami. He adapted well to the Miami life and was given the name Apekonit, or Wild Carrot. He became a trusted warrior and fought whites without hesitation. At the Battle of the Wabash, also known as St. Clair's Defeat, Wells commanded a group of Miami sharpshooters, who picked off St. Clair's artillerymen. The battle was a rout, with over 630 Americans killed and 280 wounded. Wells later said, "I killed and scalped that day until I could not raise my arms above my head."[22] He married Manwangopath (Sweet Breeze), daughter of Miami Chief Little Turtle.

In 1793, the young bilingual warrior had a change of heart and switched sides, becoming Anthony Wayne's head scout. Wells's knowledge and skills were invaluable to Wayne. On the Fallen Timbers campaign, he gave away many of Native American secrets, including where the Indians had hidden cannons taken at the Wabash. On a mission from Fort Defiance, Wells led a group all the way to Fort Miamis in current-day Maumee, Ohio. On the way back, there was an encounter with a small Indian camp and a fight. Wells was shot through the wrist, but he still made it back to Defiance with prisoners. "This enterprising young man," wrote an admiring Captain William Clark, had entered the enemy's camp and successfully brought off two prisoners, "from whome we learn the Situation and intention of the Enemey."

Almost every book and article written about the Battle of Fallen Timbers mentions Wells and the vital role he played. Ironically, though, he did not fight at Fallen Timbers. The day of the battle, he was still in Fort Defiance, nursing his shattered wrist.

Wells, as an interpreter, played a crucial role at the Treaty of Greenville. After the treaty, his father-in-law, Little Turtle, asked that he be appointed

U.S. Indian agent to the Miami. Between 1796 and 1809, he accompanied Chief Little Turtle on several trips to meet with U.S. Presidents Washington and Jefferson. Wells advocated and fought for Indian rights yet opposed the militancy of Tecumseh and his brother the Prophet. In the end, both sides accused him of betrayal and corruption.

When the War of 1812 broke out, Wells volunteered to go to Fort Dearborn and escort the garrison back to Fort Wayne. He took with him a small group of Miami warriors. Once at Fort Dearborn, he likely realized that if they left the fort, the small garrison would have little chance against the more than five hundred Native Americans surrounding them. Nevertheless, the order was to evacuate, and the order was followed. Wells marched out of the fort and, along with most of the garrison and several civilians, was killed on the sandy beach of Lake Michigan. The fate of the Miamis who were with Wells is unknown.

In 1937, sociologist Everett Stonequist published a book titled *The Marginal Man*. He described the marginal man as "one who is poised in psychological uncertainty between two or more social worlds, reflecting in his soul the discords and harmonies, repulsions and attractions of these worlds." Many historians view people on the frontier, moving between white and Native cultures, as marginal. They functioned in both worlds yet belonged to neither. Wells fits the definition, and two hundred years later, historians still argue over whether he was a hero or a victim, a selfless protector or a self-serving opportunist. In the Ohio state capitol, an enormous painting of the signing of the Treaty of Greenville hangs. On one side are the Native American leaders. Little Turtle stands holding a treaty belt in his hand. On the other side are Anthony Wayne and the Americans. Dead center, dressed in green buckskins and dividing the composition, is William Wells. He is stuck in the middle, belonging to neither side for eternity.

BLACK PARTRIDGE OF THE POTAWATOMI

On the morning of August 20, 1794, somewhere near the intersection of modern-day US Routes 24 and 475, a group of Ojibway and Potawatomi warriors checked their weapons and waited for the advance of Anthony Wayne's army. Among them was a young war chief named Black Partridge. A few hours later, the broken remains of the Native American forces were in retreat, hoping to regroup near Fort Miamis with support from the English garrison. When no help from the British appeared, the Indians had to

Black Partridge Returning His Medal, 1937 print. *Chicago History Museum.*

review their limited options. A year later, Black Partridge signed the Treaty of Greenville and pledged never to make war on the Americans again. He wore a medal given to him by Anthony Wayne as a token of his promise.

Black Partridge lived along Peoria Lake in what is now Illinois. In 1803, the United States built Fort Dearborn in current-day Chicago. At the same time, the Shawnee leader Tecumseh and his brother the Prophet were attempting to unite Native Americans against U.S. settlement. Black Partridge was a strong voice for peace and tried to keep the Potawatomi neutral. In 1812, the United States and Great Britain went to war. Most of the Potawatomis favored joining the British and driving the Americans out.

More than five hundred Potawatomis and allies surrounded Fort Dearborn. Black Partridge was on good terms with the fort's commander, Captain Heald. On the night of August 14, Black Partridge entered the fort and told the Americans what they were up against, warning them not to leave the safety of the fort. Then, according to tradition, he returned his Treaty of Greenville medal, saying,

> *Father, I come to deliver up to you the medal I wear. It was given to me by the Americans, and I have long worn it in token of our mutual friendship. Our young men are resolved to imbue their hands in the blood of the whites.*

I cannot restrain them, and I will not wear a token of peace while I am compelled to act as an enemy.

Despite Black Partridge's warning, the American commander went through with his plans to abandon the fort. On August 15, 1812, the small garrison of fifty-four regulars, accompanied by militiamen, women, children and a handful of scouts, marched away from the fort. In a brief battle, most of the Americans were killed, including the famous scout William Wells, two women and twelve children. Black Partridge intervened in the battle to save the lives of several women and children and prevent further bloodshed. According to legend, he grabbed one young woman, Margaret Helm, wife of an American officer, and dragged her into Lake Michigan, where he pretended to drown her. The ruse worked, and Margaret survived. Though he may not have known it, the young woman he saved was the daughter of an English officer who had fought alongside him at Fallen Timbers seventeen years earlier and died there.

Black Partridge spent the aftermath of the battle working as a go-between, trying to ransom white prisoners and return them to their families. At times, he even gave away his own belongings to save Americans. A few months later, he returned to his village on the Peoria and found that American rangers had burned it to the ground. This man who had worked to save Americans had now lost his daughter and a grandchild to them. He broke the promise he made at Greenville and went to war. In 1814, his band was defeated and captured. Eventually freed, he spent his last years in peace.

The young woman he saved on the shores of Lake Michigan did not forget him, and years later, her story would become a fantastic legend. Long after his death, Black Partridge would become famous and part of a modern controversy.

Monuments, Myths and Controversy

When whites are killed, it is a massacre,
but when Indians are killed, it is a fight.
—Simon Pokagon, Potawatomi writer and lecturer

Margaret McKillip Helm had an adventuresome life. Her father, a British officer, was killed at the Battle of Fallen Timbers. Then Margaret and her family barely survived the battle of Fort Dearborn, in which her husband, an

American officer, fought. She was the eldest child of Eleanor Lytle McKillip Kinzie, a former hostage of the Seneca. Margaret's mother and stepfather are considered the white founders of the city of Chicago. Margaret and Eleanor had plenty of stories to pass down to the family.

Juliette Magill Kinzie, who married Eleanor's son, took Eleanor and Margaret's stories, added a few of her own (no doubt embellishing them a bit) and wrote a book. The book, *Wau-Bun: The Early Day in the Northwest*, was published in 1856. It was a sensational bestseller that captured the nation's imagination and is still a valuable reference for anyone studying the era. It is also an over-the-top romantic saga containing not just historical inaccuracies but also historical impossibilities. For example, the story of the Battle of Fort Dearborn became the Fort Dearborn Massacre and is written in the first person from Margaret's point of view. William Wells is described as a warrior superhero dashing about on an enormous thoroughbred horse, slaying Indians left and right until he falls. Margaret recalls hearing his last words in the story, but that would have been an amazing feat considering that Margaret was almost a quarter mile away fighting for her life at the time.

Margaret's own alleged story is painted as heroic. She states that she was attacked by a crazed, tomahawk-wielding warrior. Feisty seventeen-year-old Margaret grappled with the warrior and was fighting for his knife when Black Partridge jumped in. Black Partridge blocked the warrior's tomahawk and dragged Margaret into Lake Michigan, where he pretended to drown her, thus saving her life. How much is true and how much is drama will never be known because Margaret and most of the battle's survivors were dead when *Wau-Bun* was published. This literary effort, unfortunately, became history. *Wau-Bun* has been reprinted an incredible twenty-three times and is still available.

This one-sided version of the battle angered Native Americans, starting with the Potawatomi writer Simon Pokagon, whose father, Chief Leopold Pokagon, fought in the battle. The use of the word *massacre* was especially offensive. During the frontier wars, white soldiers routinely attacked Native villages and killed women and children. From the Indian point of view, it was tragic that women and children died at Fort Dearborn, but a fight against well-armed American soldiers in a war that the U.S. started did not qualify as a massacre. Simon Pokagon interviewed Potawatomi survivors and planned to write a Native American version of the battle. Part of it appeared as an article in *Harper's Magazine* after his death in 1899.

The legend became even more exaggerated in 1893 when millionaire industrialist George Pullman commissioned a monument to the battle to be placed on the site in downtown Chicago. Danish sculptor Carl Rohl-Smith found inspiration in the dramatic version of Margaret's rescue by Black Partridge. He used Native Americans captured at Wounded Knee as models and sculpted his figures in the style of classic Rome and Greece. The sculpture portrays an evil warrior, with tomahawk raised, attacking the diminutive Margaret while she reaches for his knife. Black Partridge raises a heroic and protective arm. Margaret resembles a Greek goddess in a see-through tunic, with her hair in a classic bun. At her feet lie a fallen American soldier and a wailing baby.

The controversial Fort Dearborn Monument, by Carl Rohl-Smith, 1893. *Chicagology.com.*

The monument was controversial from the beginning. One critic described it as "sensationalist, luridly violent." Nevertheless, it became a Chicago landmark. There were even some amusing but tone-deaf postcards showing this horrifically violent scene with the cheery title "Greetings from Chicago."

In 1931, the statue was moved into the lobby of the Chicago Historical Society. In the 1980s, the statue was moved back to the original site. Native Americans and others objected to the piece, and in 1997, it was put in storage. There are still occasional campaigns to bring back the monument. As of this writing, though, this bronze memorial to false history and bad taste is quietly turning green in a damp city garage.

The statue, also known as *Black Partridge Saves Mrs. Helm*, was on public display for almost one hundred years and became, in that sense, a part of Chicago history itself. A local wag once defended the monument by claiming that generations of Chicago schoolboys looked up at Margaret's struggling, barely clad teenage body and thought, *Gee, I* really *love history*.

A first-person account of the Battle of Fort Dearborn according to Lieutenant Helm, followed by an account attributed to his wife in *Wau-Bun*, is available from Project Gutenberg.[23]

CHAPTER 4

THE INTERLOPERS

The British, the French and Everyone Caught in the Middle

Wayne Versus Simcoe: A Match Made for the Movies

When Anthony Wayne marched his army into Indian lands, enforcing the policy of the new United States, he was also pushing against the policy interests of King George III. Had Great Britain entered the conflict on behalf of its Native allies, Lieutenant Governor of Upper Canada John Graves Simcoe would have led the British forces against Wayne. It would not have been their first fight.

John Graves Simcoe is known to many people today as the villain of the TV series *Turn: Washington's Spies*. While Simcoe was not the snarky evildoer portrayed on television, he was, in fact, involved in many of the

Governor John Simcoe and Major General Anthony Wayne. *American, 1837, after a sketch by John Trumbull. Courtesy of Library and Archives Canada and Stipple Engraving.*

Canadian couple (circa 1750–80). *Anonymous. City of Montreal Document and Archive Management.*

events fictionalized in the show and was a remarkable man.

Simcoe and Wayne made careers as soldiers during the American Revolution. Simcoe led a light infantry regiment known as the Queen's Rangers. Wayne was also an advocate of light infantry tactics and, at one point, led a light infantry regiment. Both men were brave and preferred to lead from the front. Both were wounded three times during the revolution. In 1778, Simcoe became infamous for a nighttime bayonet raid on unsuspecting colonial militiamen. In 1779, Wayne became famous for leading a nighttime bayonet attack at the Battle of Stony Point. At one point during the battle of Yorktown, they were across the field from each other.

Following the war, both Simcoe and Wayne tried politics. Wayne served briefly and unsuccessfully as a U.S. congressman, and Simcoe was briefly a member of Parliament. In 1792, Simcoe was appointed lieutenant governor of Upper Canada and Wayne was appointed major general of the U.S. Army, making them commanders of potentially opposing armies.

Both men developed reputations for stern discipline and for whipping their commands into shape. Both were noted for their bad temper, and neither was squeamish about shedding blood. Skill-wise and temperament-wise, they were a close match. Both also suffered from gout and the lingering effects of war wounds. They studied each other's careers and second-guessed and anticipated each other's moves during the Fallen Timbers campaign. There was a moment at Fort Miamis when the young United States might have challenged the might of Great Britain. The moment passed, though, and further conflict between Simcoe and Wayne was averted.

A few years ago, Geoff Earnhart, former curator at the Fort Meigs Historical Site, suggested to me that if a Hollywood version of the Fallen Timbers story was made, it would have to be about the two old warhorses. Two men so much alike would be a remarkable premise on which to develop dramatic tension and suspense. The filmmakers could ignore the age and physical issues of two men and allow them to burn up the screen with their mutual contempt. Wayne would drive his army to attack Detroit just to get Simcoe. The final scene would take place on the ramparts of Detroit. Wayne and Simcoe would meet after most of their men had fallen and engage in a heroic swordfight to the death while Detroit burned. It would be really bad history, but I'd watch that movie.

Robert Pilkington: From the Maumee to Gibraltar in the Service of the King

English Second Lieutenant Robert Pilkington was twenty-five years old when he arrived in Canada. Trained as an engineer, the young officer was also a skilled mapmaker and an artist. All his skills would be tested on the frontier. Pilkington would serve the Crown until his death in 1834, after an incredible fifty-one years in uniform. He would build fortifications, buildings and other structures around the world, including gun batteries on the Rock of Gibraltar that still exist.

Remains of his work can still be seen at the site of Fort Miamis in Maumee, Ohio. In the spring of 1794, the young lieutenant traveled with Governor John Simcoe to the Maumee River, where they selected a site for a fort on the Maumee. Simcoe was convinced that Anthony Wayne's army, moving up from the Ohio River, would attack Detroit, an important and lucrative British outpost. Fort Miamis was designed to show support for the Indian confederacy fighting the Americans and to stall Wayne's advance on

The ruins of Fort Malden, Amherstburg, Ontario, overlooking the mouth of the Detroit River. *Photo by author.*

Pilkington did this drawing of the unsuccessful peace conference on the Detroit River in 1793. In his notes, he identified the Americans but none of the English or Indians. This was probably more about military intelligence than art. *Courtesy of the American Antiquarian Society.*

Detroit. In letters, Simcoe later admitted he did not expect Fort Miamis to hold if Wayne made a serious attack, but he hoped it might delay or damage Wayne's forces enough to help the Native cause and/or save Detroit. Simcoe returned to Detroit while Pilkington built Fort Miamis. Pilkington was in Maumee when Wayne arrived.

Following the Battle of Fallen Timbers, Wayne's troops moved into to the area around Fort Miamis and attempted to provoke the garrison into starting a war. Wayne was impressed by the small fortress and studied it intently. After two days, Wayne withdrew, and the British in Detroit breathed a sigh of relief.

As a result of Wayne's victory at Fallen Timbers and the Jay Treaty, signed three months later, the English had to turn over Forts Detroit and Niagara to the Americans in 1796. Pilkington was involved in building new forts in the Canadian territory, including Fort George and Fort Erie, on the Niagara River, and Fort Malden, on the Detroit River.

Pilkington remained in Canada until 1802. He designed and built fortifications and buildings throughout the Province, mapped vast regions and had a major impact on the settlement that became Toronto. In 1802, he returned to England as a captain. He fought in the Napoleonic Wars and, in 1818, became commanding royal engineer at Gibraltar, arguably the most important fortification in the British Empire. He returned to London in

1830, and in 1832, he became England's inspector general of fortifications. He died in 1834 at the age of sixty-nine. It was a long and impressive career, and it had all started on the Maumee.

The Remarkable Mrs. Simcoe: Intelligent, Sophisticated, Lovely and Alone in the Wilderness

Following the Battle of Yorktown, a seriously wounded Lieutenant Colonel John Simcoe returned to England. He was recovering at the manor of his godfather when he met his godfather's beautiful ward, Elizabeth Posthuma Gwillim. The couple were married in 1782.

When Simcoe became lieutenant governor of Canada in 1791, he brought his young wife with him to the New World. Simcoe needed to establish a capital for the new land, so he chose a site on the shores of Lake Ontario and imported loggers, carpenters and craftsmen to build a city. At first it was a collection of tents in the mud called York. Today we call it Toronto.

Elizabeth Simcoe was raised as a wealthy upper-class English girl and educated in languages, drawing and music. When she left England, she literally went from the ballrooms of Britian to the blockhouses of the frontier. She rose to the challenge and organized dances, dinners, and balls in a tent city. Her husband was in charge of what is today Ontario, as well as all points north and west. He was away much of the time. In 1794, he ordered the construction of Fort Miamis and prepared Detroit for an attack by Anthony Wayne. The small settlement at York lived in fear. England was at war with France, a new war with the United States was likely and there was a history of friction with the Native people. French Canadians, Indians and Yankees, oh my. They were surrounded by enemies and questionable friends. Elizabeth wrote in her diary that she looked out on the lake every day with fear that she would see American sails.

Self-portrait by Elizabeth Posthuma Simcoe. *Courtesy of the British Library.*

But not only did Elizabeth persevere; she also recorded it. In addition to keeping an excellent diary, Elizabeth was an artist. She left behind a series of 595 watercolor paintings of life on the frontier, including one of the Miamis (Maumee) River. Her diary has been reprinted three times, becoming an invaluable first-person source for historians.

The Simcoes returned to England in 1796 after five remarkable years. In December 2007, a statue of Elizabeth was erected in the town of Bradford West Gwillimbury, Ontario, as part of the 150th anniversary of the town's incorporation. Elizabeth and John Simcoe were buried in Wolford Chapel on the Simcoe family estate. Today, the chapel is owned by the Ontario Heritage Trust. Located in rural Devon, in South West England, the chapel is considered Canadian territory; the Canadian flag flies over the site.

Although she inherited great wealth, under the strict rules of English heraldry, Elizabeth was not a royal and not referred to as Her Ladyship. Nevertheless, looking at her art, her accomplishments and her attempts to bring grace and culture to the wilderness, many today like to think of her as Lady Elizabeth.

The Lady and the Lieutenant: Protective Friendship or Dangerous Romance?

In June 1796, Elizabeth Simcoe recorded in her diary: "Mr. Pilkington has erected a temporary room adjoining our house for the ballroom tonight." Lieutenant Robert Pilkington, the engineer who designed Fort Miamis, was a very busy man in the early days of Canada. Governor Simcoe called on him to build fortifications, barracks, docks, houses, stables and roads and to essentially create a nation's infrastructure from scratch. But no matter how busy he was, he always had time for the governor's lovely wife, Elizabeth. If the lady needed a large tent, or a canvas ballroom, built adjacent to her home, the more important structures of commerce and defense would have to wait.

The governor's duties took him all over the large province of Ontario. When the governor was away, Lieutenant Pilkington often served as escort and bodyguard to Elizabeth. There is little doubt that Pilkington was agreeable to protecting Elizabeth. The young engineer and the governor's pretty wife became good friends. They were both bright, talented, educated people and were only three years apart in age. They were both artists in a land where there was absolutely no one else like them. They were kindred souls in an extraordinary situation.

The Diary of Mrs. Simcoe. Photo by author.

This alone would have been enough for gossip, but their actions further fueled speculation. They went riding and took carriage rides together. They traded paintings and copied each other's work. The couple rode to remote areas to paint beautiful landscapes.

Their friendship has led even serious historians to wonder if the young lieutenant and the lady had a romantic affair. But if they did, they were discreet. There is no real evidence of misbehavior.

An affair would have been a very dangerous proposition. Elizabeth's husband, John Graves Simcoe, was Pilkington's commanding officer and a formidable fighting man. On one occasion during the American Revolution, his men raided a farmhouse at night and killed everyone inside, in their beds, with bayonets. He could be a very scary man.

We know from Elizabeth's diary that she considered Mr. Pilkington a very close friend. It is hard to believe that any man in the small settlement, let alone a junior officer, would dare to approach her romantically, but we'll never know for sure. What we do know is that human nature is what it is. It is possible that over two hundred years ago, a lonely young couple looked at each other while enjoying a spectacular Lake Ontario sunset and thought, "Well, this is complicated."

Alexander McKee: The Last Battle of the Great White Elk

On August 17, 1794, near what is now Riverside Park in Perrysburg, Ohio, British Indian agent Alexander McKee sat overlooking the Maumee and wrote his last will and testament, leaving the "bulk of my estate to my son Thomas and money to James Francis McKee and Catherine McKee for education."[24]

The Great Indian Council, by Lewis Foy, 1793, based on a sketch by R. Pilkington. It is believed that the British officer standing in the center is Alexander McKee, and the figure standing behind him is very likely William Caldwell, who led the Canadian volunteers at the Battle of Fallen Timbers. *Lewis Foy (1757–1825). Montreal Museum of Fine Arts.*

Meanwhile, in what is now downtown Perrysburg, McKee's wife, along with a couple of servants, made very sure they weren't observed as they secretly buried their silver plate and valuables. The cause of McKee's precautions was a large army under General Anthony Wayne approaching Roche de Boeuf near modern-day Waterville. The Americans had placed a large bounty on Colonel McKee's head, and Wayne had promised to hang him. Three days later, Wayne defeated the Native American forces at the Battle of Fallen Timbers. A day later, the Americans burned McKee's trading post to the ground. McKee avoided capture and survived the events of 1794, but he never truly recovered.

In traditional American history, Alexander McKee is often portrayed as a villain who exploited frontier violence to make a fortune. The reality is much more complicated. He was a successful businessman, masterful politician and fearless military leader. He made a fortune trading with Indians, and he lost most of it trying to help them.

McKee was born around 1735 to Scotch-Irish Indian trader Thomas McKee and his Shawnee wife, Mary. McKee was named after his grandfather, who fought in the Battle of the Boyne under William of Orange. McKee was raised in two worlds. He spent half his time with his mother living as a Shawnee and the other half as the son of a white businessman. From his mother's people, he learned Shawnee ways and how to hunt and live in the forest. His father taught him business and hired tutors to teach him math and how to read and write in English and French.

McKee was an imposing young man. He stood six foot, three inches tall at a time when the average male was five foot six. His Shawnee name was Wappemassawa, or Great White Elk. He had dark hair with a slight bit of red. Though he had Indian facial features, his skin was fair. The McKees, father and son, moved easily between white and Native American society. In a business dominated by crooks and thieves, they established a reputation for honesty. Like his father, Alexander also married a Shawnee woman.

As a young man, McKee fought for the British in the French and Indian War. At one point, he was inside a frontier fort seeking protection from Native American forces while his Shawnee wife was in a Native village outside the fort seeking protection from the settlers. He was in combat several times and shot through the shoulder once. For his service as a scout and interpreter during Pontiac's War, he was awarded an island in the Ohio River near Pittsburgh, which is still known as McKee's Rock. He built a large home on the island and named it Fairview.

McKee's business of trading with the Indians prospered. He made trips to the East Coast to meet with investors like Benjamin Franklin and spent months in the Ohio Territory maintaining friendships among the tribes. Cabin or wigwam, longhouse or boardroom, it was all the same to McKee. On the eve of the American Revolution, a Virginia land speculator named George Washington stayed several days at Fairview with McKee.

The American Revolution changed everything. McKee tried to maintain business connections and to work with the Americans at Fort Pitt. However, American suspicions and McKee's sympathy for the Native Americans made his position impossible. In 1778, McKee, Simon Girty and Matthew Elliott fled Fort Pitt and joined the British. McKee rose to the rank of colonel and fought in several campaigns with the tribes. After the war, he continued as an Indian agent for the Crown. Because of his close connections to the tribes and the respect he earned in the English government, some consider him to have been the most powerful man in British North America.

The day of the Battle of Fallen Timbers, McKee was somewhere outside of Fort Miamis roaming the woods. Though he took no part in the fighting, he observed and spoke to several participants. He wrote what today we would call an after-action report and sent it to English Governor Simcoe. After the battle, Wayne burned Indian villages, storehouses, and fields up and down the Maumee. With no food supplies, the Indians faced a very grim winter. McKee worked tirelessly to get food to the Indians and spent from his own pocket. The British government failed to support its allies, and many starved. The following summer, the Indians went to Fort Greenville and made peace with the United States. McKee moved to Canada and continued to work as an Indian agent. He was now in his sixties. War wounds, a life lived between two worlds and heartbreak took their toll. He died in his bed of rheumatoid arthritis on January 15, 1799, the same year as his onetime business associate George Washington.[25]

Several "history" books and novels have claimed McKee died after a pet deer playfully butted him in the buttocks. Even bestselling Ohio author Allan Eckert repeated the story that the deer's antlers pierced an artery, causing McKee to bleed to death. This myth probably originated in a crude frontier "horn in the buttocks" sex reference. For some reason, the Americans who despised McKee delighted in attributing sexual adventures to him. There is even a legend that he had an affair with Tecumseh's sister Tecumapease. Tecumapease was a leader in tribal affairs and much admired, but it is highly unlikely that there was ever any romance between the two. Another remarkable woman McKee was linked to was Nonhelema of the Shawnee. Nonhelema was the sister of McKee's friend Chief Cornstalk, who was murdered by white settlers in 1777. Nonhelema was intelligent, bilingual and a power player in Indian affairs. She went to war with the men and fought like a man. At over six feet, she was very tall. American accounts sometimes portray her as a freakishly large, unattractive woman. Indian and British accounts describe a strong, slender woman of exceptional beauty. Again, while McKee and Nonhelema were acquainted, there is nothing that suggests a romance. Despite attempts in American legend to portray McKee as a ladies' man, or even gay, it appears he was faithful to both his first wife and, after her death, his second wife, Edna Yellow Britches. Both women were Shawnee.

American historians have long insisted on branding McKee a disloyal traitor. The fact is, though, that he was extremely loyal—to both his father's king and his mother's people.

P.S. McKee returned to his trading post after Wayne's army left, and it is assumed he recovered his buried silver. Please don't go digging up downtown Perrysburg.

Thunder from the North: Canadians at Fallen Timbers

On the warm morning of August 20, 1794, near the current-day intersection of Interstate 475 and State Route 24, a group of mounted Kentucky militiamen rode toward a concealed Indian battle line. With the first shots, two Kentuckians fell dead from their horses, and their comrades retreated. Some of the Indians advanced and ran into American skirmishers. Within minutes, both sides were engaged in the Battle of Fallen Timbers. To Wayne's north, fifty to one hundred Canadian volunteers waited in position alongside the Wyandots and Odawa. As the sound of musket and rifle fire rippled up and down Wayne's front the Fourth Legion moved north to protect the American left flank. The Canadians waited until the Americans were well within range, and then they unleashed a tremendous volley.[26] The thunder of that volley was heard everywhere on the battlefield. It startled the Americans because it obviously came from a well-trained and disciplined force. In the view of some historians, that volley marked the first shots fired by the Canadian Armed Forces on foreign soil.

The Canadians were there in an unofficial capacity. It was what we might call today a covert operation. The English government wanted to support the Native forces but could not commit regular troops without starting a war, so its solution was to field a company of Detroit-area militiamen, along with a French-Canadian unit, as "volunteers." These volunteers wore no uniforms, carried no flags and were told to dress as Indians. They were under the command of Colonel William Caldwell.

The Canadians, Wyandots and Odawa suffered heavy losses. They fought a bloody rearguard action: withdrawing, reforming, returning fire, withdrawing, reforming and returning fire. At least six of the Canadians were killed in the fight. Many more were wounded. Among the Canadian dead were Captain Daniel McKillip, Captain Daniel Fields, Charles Munger and Charles Smith. McKillip was born in Quebec and had fought in the American Revolution. He left behind a young wife and a daughter. He was described as "a thriving, rising, industrious man of very great use in his settlement." Smith was the clerk of the court for Detroit.

Munger, or Monger, was originally an American. During the Revolution, he was captured at the Battle of Ruddell's Station in Kentucky. He was taken to Detroit as a hostage and decided to stay and settle on the Canadian side. His son married the daughter of the infamous Simon Girty. Many years later, the historian Lyman Draper interviewed Sarah Girty Munger and recorded the following account of her father-in-law's death at Fallen Timbers:

> *Charles Munger (the father of Mrs. Munger's husband Joseph Munger) was with the British & Indians in Wayne's Fight in 1794—had his thigh broken by a bullet—was sitting on a log, when an American officer rode up & Munger said he was a white man—the officer remarked that he could recognize none such with the Indians, & cut him down.*[27]

Xavier Allen of Canada's Essex and Kent Scottish Regiment pays his respects to the fallen on the Fallen Timbers Battlefield. *Photo by author.*

The participation of the Canadian militia marked a critical moment in American and Canadian history. So why has this story been ignored for over two hundred years? Three major reasons have emerged, the first of which has to do with the nature of covert operations. For many years, covert operations were considered dirty or dishonorable. Beginning in the twentieth century, society began to recognize that covert operations are a vital part of war and that the sacrifices of the men and women involved are every bit as worthy of recognition as the sacrifices of those involved in "official" wars.

The second reason is the racial attitudes of the frontier. Many on the American side saw Indians as savages, and they saw anyone who fought with them as a renegade or an outlaw. These attitudes lasted until very recently.

The third reason this moment has been ignored is Canadian history itself. Canada was not a self-governing nation until 1867. Therefore, since in 1794, Canada was not a nation, some argue that the volunteers at Fallen Timbers were British, not Canadian. I would argue that they were not fighting for Britain but for Canada. These were not British regulars like the Twenty-Fourth Regiment of Foot stationed at Fort Miamis. These were Canadians fighting under Canadian leaders to defend their home, Canada. Colonel Richard England (commander of Fort Detroit) wrote in a letter to Governor John Graves Simcoe, "I took upon me to assemble the Militia of the Counties of Essex and Kent in consequence of the rapid advance of the Army under General Wayne."[28]

I believe that the volunteers fighting near Monclova Road that hot August morning undertook the first military action of the Canadian armed forces. As for the men who fell, there has been speculation, but no evidence, that their remains were sent home. It is more likely they were buried in unmarked graves somewhere between the Fallen Timbers battlefield and Fort Miamis. According to English tradition, when a fallen soldier is buried in a foreign land, that patch of soil becomes a part of England. Somewhere in modern-day Maumee, Ohio, are six spots of soil that are forever Canada.

Between a Rock and a Hard Place: French Canadians at Fallen Timbers

Historians speak of the Battle of Fallen Timbers as a conflict between the Native Americans and the young American nation. Occasionally, the British and Loyalist supporters playing a supporting role as allies of the Natives are mentioned. A fourth, seldom mentioned, group was also involved. Sixty to seventy French Canadians participated in the Battle of Fallen Timbers. French Canadians are a distinct cultural group with its own language, religion, customs and politics.

The French had fought the English colonists thirty-four years earlier for control of North America and lost. What we call the French and Indian War was a brutal affair that left hateful memories. The French in America were not trusted by the Americans or the English. It was an uneasy situation. Frenchtown on the River Raisin (present-day Monroe, Michigan) was actually founded in defiance of English laws. While Frenchtown was built on land claimed by the United States, its people were considered subjects of England, which was at war with France. In 1794, as Anthony Wayne made his advance toward the heart of the Indian confederacy, British Governor John Simcoe needed men to defend Detroit. So he called on the French. One group of twenty to thirty men were conscripted as forced labor to help build Fort Miamis. Others were called to serve in combat roles as Canadian militiamen. Somewhere between fifty and seventy Canadian Militia men (English and French) took part in the battle as allies of the Indians. Since it was an unofficial or covert operation, they were dressed and painted as Indians. Half of this militia was French.

What separated the Canadiens (French) from the Canadians (English) was their relationship with the Native Americans. The French dealt openly and moved freely among the tribes, often intermarrying. French fur traders lived with the Indians and quickly learned their language and customs. When the French took the field at Fallen Timbers, they may have been acting under the authority of the English Crown, but they were fighting for their Indian brothers.

According to Monroe native and researcher Dennis Au, there were thirty-seven militiamen under the command of Captain Charles Réaume at the Battle of Fallen Timbers. The Canadian militia were on the Native American right flank with the Wyandots. When the Indian line collapsed, the Canadians and Wyandots fought a bloody rearguard action covering the retreat. In recognition of their bravery, Governor Simcoe proposed that every man in the company be awarded "one hundred pounds in specie" (cash).

While the French militia preformed heroically on the battlefield, the French laborers at Fort Miamis did not. The French men working on the earthworks at Fort Miamis realized that standing between Wayne's approaching army and the guns of the redcoat fort was not a healthy choice. They quit work and fled, earning the scorn of the fort's commander, British Major Campbell.

Reenactor Joel Berg portraying Antoine LaSalle. *Photo by author.*

One of Réaume's men, fur trader Antoine Lasselle (or LaSalle), was captured by Wayne's troops. According to the story Antoine was too fat to run, so he tried to hide. Wayne wanted to hang him, but a court of inquiry spared him. Wayne eventually released him on the condition that he support the United States, recruit other Frenchmen and encourage his

Native American friends and associates to make peace. LaSalle kept his word. It soon became known that the River Raisin French were encouraging the Native Americans to sign a treaty with Wayne.

The story of the French was quickly forgotten. The American victors were not inclined to recognize those who opposed them, and the English, battling Napoleon in Europe, soon forgot their French allies in America. Three years after the battle, Captain Réaume called on the new British commander at Fort Malden and was refused admittance because, as a Frenchman, he was not considered a gentleman and therefore not fit company for an officer.

Though much of their history was ignored and their culture discouraged, the French in North America did not go away. The stories of people like LaSalle and Réaume have survived largely through the efforts of their descendants. That may be why the official motto of French Quebec is "Je me souviens": I remember.

Simon Girty at the Battle of Fallen Timbers: Even Bad Guys Take a Sick Day Once in a While

The notorious Simon Girty was with the Native Americans before the Battle of Fallen Timbers and in the days immediately after the battle. According to one tradition, British Indian agents Simon Girty, Alexander McKee and Matthew Elliott sat on horses atop a high hill in current-day Maumee and watched the battle. The problem, though, is that there is no such hill in Maumee. McKee was in the vicinity of the battle that day, but when he reported back to Fort Miamis, he came in from the river in a canoe. We don't know where Girty was the day of the battle, but we can make a pretty good guess. At this point in his life, Girty was suffering from blackouts and severe headaches caused by an old head wound. He self-medicated with liberal amounts of alcohol. Due to either a blackout or a hangover, he was most likely passed out on the floor of an Indian dwelling during the battle. It was a sad ending to a flamboyant and legendary career.

Girty was the most feared and hated man on the Ohio frontier. The United States government put a bounty on his head, which eventually reached what was, for the time, the incredible amount of $1,000. When that failed, the United States even added a lifetime pension. No one collected, though, and Girty died of old age in Canada. Frontier legend portrayed him as a bloodthirsty savage who delighted in torture and murder. Frontier mothers would warn their children, "If you don't behave, Simon Girty will get you."

Simon Girty's powder horn and the cane he used as an old man. *Fort Malden Museum, Amherstburg, Ontario. Photo by author.*

Girty was a product of frontier violence. In his lifetime, he fought in five wars, was wounded several times and no doubt killed men in combat. He was not, however, the monster he is portrayed as. There is no legitimate account of Girty ever harming any prisoner, let alone a woman or a child. When the American Revolution broke out, he was more comfortable fighting for the English and the Indians. Many in the colonies considered him a traitor, though the British would argue that the colonists rebelling against the king were the real traitors. We have documented accounts of Girty ransoming many white prisoners, sometimes at his own expense. On several occasions, Girty intervened to save white men condemned to death. Girty was a man of contradictions. It is believed that in addition to English, he spoke French and at least nine Native American languages, yet he could not read or write in any of them; he couldn't even sign his name.

Three factors created the myth of Girty the savage. First, he was present for some of the most horrible episodes of the frontier wars. He was present but unable to do anything when American Colonel William Crawford was burned at the stake. Secondly, people at war vilify their opponents. The enemy must be the bad guy, or your reason for fighting becomes questionable. This is especially important when the opposition is very good at what they do. The third factor was Girty himself. He had a sense of drama and purpose. At some point, he realized that being perceived as scary helped him do his job. If your job is to be bad, you might as well be the baddest man in the forest. He bragged about and exaggerated his own fierceness.

This was especially true in the case of the Moravian Christian missionaries. Girty's mission to encourage and coordinate Indian resistance was the opposite of the missionaries' goal to pacify the Indians and encourage them to accept white settlement. Even by eighteenth-century standards, harming a missionary was not acceptable, so Girty could not touch the missionaries, even when he knew they were feeding intelligence to the Americans. However, that did not stop him from terrorizing them every chance he got. Missionary David Heckewelder wrote on one occasion,

> *Girty behaved like a madman…swore the most horrid oaths respecting us…*[saying] *that he never would leave the house, until he had split our heads in two, and made our brains stick to the walls of the room.…He appeared like a host of evil spirits…this White beast in human form… this wicked white savage.*

While Girty never actually harmed a missionary, these accounts of his terrifying and shocking behavior were written into American history.

Girty also dressed the part. He wore a red bandanna pirate-style, which made him easily recognizable. White hostage Oliver Spencer described him in 1792 in this way:

> *He wore the Indian costume, but without any ornament; and his silk handkerchief while it supplied the place of a hat, hid an unsightly wound in his forehead. On each side in his belt, were stuck silver-mounted pistols, and at his left hung a short, broad dirk, serving occasionally the uses of a knife.*[29]

Following the Battle of Fallen Timbers, Girty's health went into serious decline. In addition to the head wound, he suffered a debilitating leg injury, developed arthritis and lost his vision. During the War of 1812, the blind old man had to flee the American invasion of Canada. Despite his feebleness, there is an American legend that he died fighting at the Battle of the Thames alongside Tecumseh. It is quite a picture: Girty in his red bandanna, a pistol in each hand, standing beside the great Tecumseh, facing the thundering hoofs of a calvary charge. The irony is that this is exactly the kind of ending Girty would have liked.

Catherine Malott Girty, the Most Beautiful Woman in Detroit

When the Battle of Fallen Timbers is discussed, the people most directly affected are often ignored. I'm talking about the women, wives and widows of the men who fought there. The stories of the women of the frontier are every bit as interesting and sometimes as heartbreaking as those of the men they were with. One of my favorites is Catherine Malott Girty, wife of the notorious Simon Girty. Simon Girty, as an interpreter and combat leader, fought with the Native Americans during the American Revolution and the Northwest Indian Wars and played a role in the Battle of Fallen Timbers. He was feared and hated by the Americans. Until recently, the story of his wife, Catherine, has been overshadowed by the exploits of the great renegade himself.

Catherine Malott was born in 1764 in Maryland to Peter and Sarah Malott. The Malotts were of French descent. In March 1778, despite the war raging up and down the frontier, Peter decided to move his family to Kentucky. The Malotts and another family loaded their belongings onto two flatboats and began the journey down the Ohio River. On March 22, they were attacked by a party of Delawares. Peter was in the front boat with the livestock and escaped. Fourteen-year-old Catherine was with her mother and siblings in the rear boat; they were captured. Two people in Catherine's boat, including a little girl, were shot and killed in the brief fight. Catherine told her grandchildren that the girl was sitting in her lap when she was killed.

The hostages were divided up and taken deep into the Ohio country. Sarah, a formidable woman, eventually made it to British-held Detroit. Once in Detroit, she somehow managed to raise money and recover all her children except Catherine. When the war ended in 1782, Sarah hired Simon Girty to find her lost daughter. He found her in a Delaware village on the Mad River. The girl who was lost at fourteen was now a survivor and a woman. Girty was obliged to return Catherine to her mother in Detroit, but on the long journey from the Mad River to Detroit, something happened. The hard-drinking, hard-fighting, forty-year-old bachelor fell in love.

Much of Girty's life is still argued about and debated, but there is one area of agreement: he was not a womanizer. If he had affairs of the heart, he was very careful. There are no broken hearts, unclaimed children or ugly romances in his story. There is, indeed, little evidence of romance in Simon's life at all until he met Catherine. The pretty Catherine created a stir in Detroit. One hundred years later, Dr. George Ranck, writing in the *Magazine of American History*, claimed that Catherine had many admirers among the soldiers at Fort Detroit. Still, "she turned away from her red-coated and more civilized admirers and accepted the strange and notorious white savage." In 1784, twenty-year-old Catherine married forty-three-

Pocahontas. Artist unknown.

year-old Simon. The ceremony was performed by a clergyman and is the only recorded instance of Girty ever being in a church.

Catherine was taller than most women of her time, probably around five foot seven. She had dark hair, dark eyes and a "womanly figure." Strong and slender, she was described as "the most beautiful woman in Detroit." In what sounds like a movie cliché, the deadliest man on the frontier married the most beautiful woman in the territory. In the Old Northwest, they were what we would call today a power couple.

There is no record of how Sarah felt about having Simon Girty as a son-in-law. We do know that her husband returned to Maryland and, thinking Sarah was dead, married a young woman named Rachel. When he learned Sarah was alive, he sent her a letter saying she could return and make a life with him and his wife. Sarah was not impressed. She stayed in Detroit and claimed land that would later become the affluent suburb of Grosse Pointe, Michigan.

Girty had a farm near Amherstburg, Ontario, given to him in recognition of his service to the Crown. The Girtys settled there, and Catherine ran it. The first years of their marriage seemed to pass agreeably. Simon was often gone on extended missions into the Ohio Territory. Their first child died at birth. Catherine bore four more children: Nancy (1786), Thomas, (1788), Sarah (1792) and Prideaux, born in 1796.

The Girtys' life changed in 1796, after the birth of Prideaux, when the Americans took control of Detroit and Simon came home for good. Simon's health began to deteriorate as the result of several old wounds and his dependance on alcohol to deal with the pain. He had a head wound that caused severe headaches, blackouts and mood swings.

The age difference became a problem. Catherine was a woman in her prime tied to a deteriorating warhorse. In 1798, she left. Simon's critics have long since spun tails of physical abuse and painted Catherine as a victim. There is no evidence of physical abuse, though Simon, when drinking, was obnoxious. There are many indications that leaving was a

Above: *The Chief's Daughter*, by John Gadsby Chapman.

Opposite: *Spotted Fawn*, by George Winters. At various times, it's been claimed that the women in the paintings *Pocahontas*, *The Chief's Daughter* and *Spotted Faun* are Catherine Girty. Unfortunately, they are not; there is no known portrait of Catherine.

positive move on Catherine's part. She needed a break. When she left, she took their youngest child, who was an infant, with her. The older children stayed with Simon, who, despite his illness and drinking, cared for them and continued to work for the government as an interpreter.

The Girtys suffered the loss of another child. Their oldest son, Thomas, fought with the British army in 1812. During a battle outside of Detroit, he collapsed and died while carrying a wounded comrade from the field. Almost completely blind, arthritic and lame, Simon Girty had to flee the American army. He returned home in 1815, and Catherine moved home to care for him. On February 18, 1818, Girty died an old man with Catherine by his side.

Catherine lived another thirty-four years, dying on January 2, 1852, at the age of eighty-eight. The most beautiful women in Detroit never remarried and spent her last years as a doting grandmother in quiet obscurity.

A Touch of Evil: Matthew Elliott, British Indian Agent

Early December 1812 was cold. A small boat quietly worked its way down the Maumee River, headed toward Lake Erie and Canada. A man in the bow worked to break the ice that was forming on the river, while others rowed and tried to keep their hands from freezing. In the center of the boat lay a corpse wrapped in a shroud. Accompanying the dead man was a hard-looking old man with long, snow-white hair. Matthew Elliott was over seventy years old. He had been at war for almost fifty years. Now war had claimed his son's life. Colonel Elliott was taking his boy home.

On December 17, 1812, Alexander Elliott was buried in Amherstburg, Ontario, near the Elliott estate. Alexander was his father's oldest son. Though his mother was Native American and his father illiterate, he was educated. Just before the war broke out, he passed the bar and was licensed to practice law. His family had high hopes for him. When Alexander died, all those hopes ended. As soon as he was buried, his father went back to war.

Matthew Elliott was a polarizing figure in his day and remains controversial. American history traditionally paints him as a murderous villain and minimizes his role in the Indian wars. Canadian history notes that he fought tirelessly for the Crown but also alienated his British superiors. Elliott was dedicated to the Native American cause but shamelessly used his position as an Indian agent to become wealthy. He owned one of the largest and most successful farms in North America, but he built it with slaves. It is almost impossible to separate the good from the evil in the story of Matthew Elliott. One thing both his supporters and detractors agree on is that he had a bad temper and was easily angered.

Colonel Matthew Elliott's coat from the 1770s was redone in the style of 1812. He may have worn it during the Fallen Timbers campaign. *Fort Malden Museum, Amherstburg, Ontario. Photo by author.*

Elliott was born in Ireland and immigrated to America around 1761. He went west and worked as an Indian trader. He served under Colonel Bouquet during Pontiac's War. Elliott lived with the Native Americans in the Ohio Territory and took a Wyandotte wife. His business prospered until the outbreak of the American Revolution. Described as a short, pug-nosed Irishman, he did not inspire trust. When the Americans requested his trade goods for the war effort, he got angry and refused. He then approached the English at Fort Detroit, who decided he was an American spy and clapped him in irons. He was sent to Quebec, where he managed to talk his way out of the spy charge and was allowed to return to Pittsburgh.

The Americans still did not trust him, so he got angry, and in 1778, he stepped into history as part of the treasonous trio of Simon Girty, Alexander McKee and Matthew Elliott. The trio fled Pittsburgh and joined the British Indian Department. The flamboyant Girty, with his command of Native American languages and fearlessness in combat, became the most famous. McKee, with his talent for organization and command, also became famous. Elliott, on the other hand, was seen as an Irish stereotype.

Early American writers referred to him as bad-tempered, foulmouthed and frequently drunk. While the Americans dismissed him, he was winning the respect of Native Americans by fighting with them in engagement after bloody engagement.

Throughout the horror and hardship of war, Elliott kept his business as an Indian trader going. In fact, he added to it, with plunder taken in raids on American settlements. For his service, the Crown gave him land near what is today Amherstburg, Ontario. In 1784, he built a beautiful home on the Detroit River. His friendship with the Indians allowed him to make favorable land deals and enlarge his holdings.

Elliott continued, along with Girty and McKee, to work as an Indian agent and fought in several battles during the Northwest Indian War. In the summer of 1793, he hosted a delegation of Americans in his home, who attempted to make a peace treaty with the tribes. He was in the area the day of the Battle of Fallen Timbers but did not take part. Following the Treaty of Greenville, Elliott continued to build his business while working as an Indian agent. When McKee's health went into decline, Elliott was appointed to his position as superintendent of Indian affairs. It is believed that Elliott used his position to help himself to goods and funds intended for the Indians.

The commandant at Fort Malden (Amherstburg), Captain Hector McLean, had an intense dislike of Elliott. In a letter to James Green, the military secretary at Quebec, he wrote:

> *He* [Elliott] *lives…in the greatest affluence at an expense of above a thousand a year. He possesses an extensive farm not far from the garrison stock'd with about six or seven hundred head of cattle &…employs fifty or sixty persons constantly about his house & farm, chiefly slaves.…How his wealth had been accumulated…is well known.*[30]

McLean's complaints resulted in Elliott losing his job. He continued to try and get his job as Indian agent back, even traveling to London to lobby. Meanwhile, his farm, which was in effect a plantation, grew and despite government pressure, he refused to free any slaves.[31] His enemies (of which he had many) claimed he was a brutal slave owner. Despite his enemies, he prospered. In 1810, he married a very young white woman named Sarah Donovan and was elected to the Provincial House of Assembly. While his son by his first wife was finishing his education in Montreal, he had two infant sons by Sarah. At this time, he owned over four thousand acres of land and was very wealthy.

When the War of 1812 broke out, the British needed a person the Indians trusted, and that was Matthew Elliott. He got his job as Indian agent back and a commission in the Essex militia as a colonel. Elliot and his son Alexander were with Tecumseh when the Indians and the British captured Detroit. They were part of the unsuccessful attack on Fort Wayne. In the fall, they were camped on the Maumee and scouting the advancing American army when, on November 22, 1812, a group of Indians under the command of young Alexander encountered a group of Shawnees scouting for the Americans on Turkey Foot Creek in what is today Henry County. The Shawnees were led by the famous Chief Spemica Lawba, also known as Captain Logan. Alexander's party captured the Shawnees, but then they got careless. Logan saw an opportunity to attempt an escape and grabbed a gun. In the fight that ensued, Alexander was killed, and Logan was mortally wounded. Elliott recovered his son's body and returned to Amherstburg.

Elliott was soon back in the field. He was with the Native American forces who defeated the Americans at the River Raisin in January. He was also there a day later when an undisciplined group of Indians brutally killed most of the wounded American soldiers. This is where the rumors began. The story was that not only did the grief-stricken and angry old man fail to prevent the atrocities, but he also encouraged them.

In May, Elliott was with Tecumseh at the siege of Fort Meigs. On the morning of May 5, a company of Kentucky militiamen under the command of Colonel William Dudley were defeated near the present-day site of the Maumee Library. Survivors were taken to the ruins of Fort Miamis a mile away. Again, an unruly group of Indians began tormenting and killing the prisoners. Tecumseh and Elliot arrived on the scene and stopped the killings. Some accounts credit Elliott for bravely supporting Tecumseh, while others say he did so reluctantly. Commander of British forces General Henry Procter maintained that Elliot encouraged the Indians to kill the prisoners and bore much of the responsibility for their deaths.[32]

In the fall of 1813, American General William Henry Harrison took back Detroit and invaded Canada. Fort Malden at Amherstburg was abandoned. A group of Kentucky militia ransacked Elliott's farm. His young wife fled with their most valuable belongings in several wagons. While Sarah Elliott escaped, the Americans did capture and loot the wagons. Elliott fought with Tecumseh at the Battle of the Thames, where the Shawnee leader was killed. Despite the death of Tecumseh, the defeat at the Thames and the loss of his farm and all his possessions, Elliott managed to move the

The Elliott homestead, built 1784; photo circa 1912. *Parks Canada Agency, Fort Malden National Historic Site.*

Indians under his command east. In December, Elliott and his warriors helped take Fort Niagara.

While fighting on the Niagara frontier, Elliott's age finally caught up to him. He took ill and died of natural causes on May 7, 1814. He was believed to have been seventy-five years old. Gordon Drummond, the British administrator of Upper Canada, stated, "His Majesty has lost one of his most faithful and zealous servants."[33]

Elliott's young widow and sons inherited his house and property and eventually sold it. In the late nineteenth century, it was a historic attraction but not for anything Elliott did. Escaped American slave Eliza Harris stayed there briefly. Her story inspired Eliza's story in Harriet Beecher Stowe's novel *Uncle Tom's Cabin*. For a while, the Elliott house was known as Eliza's Cottage. Ironically, the slave owner's house was considered a monument to the Underground Railroad. The house fell into disrepair in the early twentieth century and collapsed in the 1940s.

Elliott helped build what is today Canada. Born in obscure poverty, he rose to great wealth and power. He was respected and trusted by Native Americans even while he stole from them. He was a friend and supporter of Tecumseh. He was a war hero who may have been a war criminal. He was an unapologetic and brutal slave owner at a time when English society was moving to abolish the institution. While some historians would consider this a mixed legacy, that is a hard position to defend. In Amherstburg, there is a museum dedicated to the Underground Railroad and the history of

African people in Canada. In the museum is a piece of an ancient black locust tree with an iron ring embedded in it. It was found on the Elliott property. Enslaved human beings were once tied to this ring and whipped.

For many years, a historic marker stood on the site of Elliot's farm south of Amherstburg, noting his life achievements. Questions were raised about the propriety of honoring a notorious slave owner. As of 2023, the marker has disappeared. We can argue whether that is the right or wrong way to handle troubling history, but there is one thing we can say with certainty: Elliott would be very angry.

William Caldwell of the Queens Rangers: "A Very, Very Odd but Very Gallant Fellow"

People who have studied the Battle of Fallen Timbers believe that the Native American confederacy had a sound battle plan. A group of warriors would engage the Americans as they advanced along the trail (current day Route 24) and then fall back. The pursuing Americans would run into a force of warriors fighting from a tangled mass of timber left by a recent tornado (just west of current-day I-475). When the American army was bogged down in the fallen timbers, a force made up mostly of Wyandotte and Canadian would come from the north (just south of current-day Monclova Road) and hammer Wayne's left flank. The attack on the left would drive the Americans toward the river and force them down the hill onto the floodplain. The Americans would find themselves exposed in a grassy kill zone. The Native alliance on the high ground would easily destroy them.

Unfortunately for the Indians, on the morning of August 20, they did not have enough people on the field to successfully execute the plan, and Wayne refused to be flanked. Instead of being a hammer, the Canadians and Wyandottes found themselves under an intense attack and fighting a desperate and bloody rearguard action. They suffered heavy losses. Commanding the Canadian "volunteers" was Lieutenant Colonel William Caldwell of the Queens Rangers.

> *A few days after the battle Colonel R.G. England, Commander of Fort Detroit, wrote Canadian Governor John Graves Simcoe. "That very very odd but very gallant fellow, Lieutenant Colonel Caldwell, who early went out to Fort Miamis with nearly sixty men from the new settlement, was in the action, I believe, with all his people, and as I am informed very*

> *gallantly with the Wyndots only, covered the Indians when retreating, and bore the heaviest part of the action against the Light Cavalry without moving for a long time.*[34]

Caldwell's actions that day were consistent with his behavior as a soldier. His military record shows a man who was competent, brave and incredibly cool in combat. William Caldwell the warrior was fierce, commanding and heroic. William Caldwell the civilian was less than competent. What Colonel England called odd, others saw as obnoxious. His off-putting "odd" behavior is probably why we do not hear more about his heroics. It seems that a lot of people who came to power in Canada simply did not like William Caldwell.

Caldwell was born in Northern Ireland around 1750. He came to America in 1773 and soon found himself fighting on the frontier. He was an officer in the Virginia Militia and fought in Lord Dunmore's War and the Battle of Point Pleasant in 1774. When the American Revolution broke out in 1775, Caldwell stayed with Lord Dunmore's Loyalist forces and fought the Americans. He was badly wounded in the storming of Norfolk, Virginia. When he recovered, he went to Fort Niagara and became a captain in the infamous frontier Loyalist force known as Butler's Rangers.

Butler's green-clad rangers fought up and down the New York and Pennsylvania frontier in a war where atrocities were gruesome and common on both sides. According to the Dictionary of Canadian Biography, "In the Rangers' campaigns Caldwell was 'a very active Partisan,' according to the fort's commandant. He led, rather than ordered, his troops into battle and he demonstrated a ruthlessness that the Americans would remember."[35]

In 1778, Caldwell and fifty rangers were sent to Fort Detroit. He fought several engagements on the Ohio frontier, including the 1782 Battle of Upper Sandusky. In keeping with his style of leading from the front, he was wounded on the first day of the fight. A bullet went through one leg and lodged in the other. Command of the rangers then fell to Lieutenant John Turney. In two days of fighting, the Native American forces and their British allies trounced the American army, captured the American commander and forced the Americans to flee for their lives. While everyone else was celebrating the victory, Caldwell summoned Lieutenant Turney to his recovery tent, where he angrily chewed him out. Caldwell was upset that any Americans had escaped.[36]

Caldwell recovered from his wounds quickly, and a few months later, he led his rangers at the Battle of Blue Licks Kentucky. At Blue Licks, the Indians and their British allies destroyed an American army that included the famous Daniel Boone. When the war ended, Caldwell was rewarded with land in what would become Amherstburg, Canada. The government, realizing ex-military men were useful on the frontier, assisted Caldwell in bringing many of his ex-rangers to the area. He formed a trading company with the infamous Matthew Elliott as a partner. They energetically traded with an American company and then failed to pay their debts and sank both firms. Caldwell and Elliott were accused of corruption, and the Americans tried unsuccessfully to collect from them. Fortunately for Caldwell, he was successful in getting land grants from the Indians. His ability to acquire land offset his business failings. He is credited with founding a community on Lake Erie that was called the New Settlement.

When Anthony Wayne and the Americans moved north, threatening British Canada, Caldwell was quick to reform his ranger company and move to reinforce the Native American confederacy. Following the Battle of Fallen Timbers, Caldwell returned home to Amherstburg. Despite his argumentative nature and dubious business ethics, he married the daughter of Jacques Baby, one of Detroit's leading citizens, and had eight children. He also had a son, Billy, from a previous marriage to a Mohawk woman. When the War of 1812 broke out, Caldwell and his four sons by Suzanne Baby took the field as rangers. They were at the Battle of the Thames when Tecumseh was killed. They went on to fight at the Battles of Longwood, Chippawa and Lundy's Lane and the siege of Fort Erie.

On the death of Matthew Elliott in 1814, Caldwell was appointed head of the Indian Department. In this role, he soon quarreled with military, civilian and Indian leaders. This "odd" man was accused of nepotism and theft in office, which he hotly denied, even though he did appoint his white sons to lucrative positions. In 1815, he was removed as head of the Indian Department and replaced by his eldest son, the part-Mohawk Billy, who had turned against him.

Caldwell spent the rest of his life rebuilding the farm the Americans destroyed in 1813 and developing the community of Amherstburg. Despite almost fifty years of war and several wounds, he died an old man in 1822. He converted to Catholicism late in life and donated land in Amherstburg for both the Catholic and Anglican churches. The old soldier was still covering all flanks. When he donated the land to build Christ Church in Amherstburg, he stipulated that a pew be marked and reserved for his use. The church still stands, and there is still a pew reserved for Lieutenant Colonel William Caldwell.

The Chief's Daughter and the Fair-Haired Englishman: Sally Blue Jacket and Charles Shortt

Since the beginning of history, soldiers have romanced local girls in foreign lands. Sometimes lasting relationships are formed, but more often than not, the brutal reality is "love 'em and leave 'em." Wartime romances can happen anywhere, even on the banks of the Maumee River.

Lieutenant Colonel William Charles Shortt. This picture was given to Colonel Webb C. Hayes of Fremont, Ohio, by a descendant of William Taylor Peter Shortt. The painting was done while Colonel Shortt was serving in the Twenty-Fourth Regiment of Foot. *Courtesy of the Hayes Presidential Center, Fremont, Ohio.*

In early 1794, the British built Fort Miamis, in what is today Maumee, Ohio, to support Native American forces and to protect Detroit from the advance of American forces under Anthony Wayne. A thirty-year-old English redcoat noticed an unusually light-skinned and lovely girl among the Indians camped near the fort. Ensign Shortt was the son of an English officer and educated at Eton. The teenager who caught his eye inherited her fair complexion from her mother's father, Jacques Baby, a French trader in Detroit. In every other way, she was Shawnee. Her name was Sally Blue Jacket, daughter of Weyapiersenwah, or as we know him, Blue Jacket, war chief of the Shawnee.[37]

Spring and early summer of 1794 was an exciting time on the Ohio frontier. Anthony Wayne's Legion of the United States was slowly moving north. The English were working to finish Fort Miamis and prepare their defenses. Blue Jacket, Little Turtle of the Miami and the principal chiefs of the Ohio tribes were feverishly trying to hold their alliance together, find more warriors, convince the English to support them, harass Wayne's advance and consider peace offers—all at the same time.

Shortly before the Battle of Fallen Timbers, Ensign Shortt was promoted to Captain Shortt. The handsome redcoat must have seemed quite dashing to young Sally. Sally was raised in what by frontier standards was a sophisticated household. When not at war, Blue Jacket was a successful trader. His sons were educated. He lived in a cabin, and visitors remarked that his table was set with finer plate and silverware than most white homes'. Some of the most important people of the day, French, English, American and Indian, were visitors in the Blue Jacket home.

The English at Fort Miamis did not support the Indians during the Battle of Fallen Timbers. While the relationship between the British and the Native Americans was severely damaged, the relationship between Captain Shortt and Sally thrived. Though we have yet to find any English record of the occasion, Blue Jacket family tradition says they were married. In 1796, most likely in Detroit, they had a son, Thomas.[38] Then the unthinkable happened. Captain Shortt was recalled to England and abandoned his Shawnee family.

Eventually, Sally married a Detroit-area trader named Wilson, who raised Thomas Shortt as his own. The Blue Jacket and Wilson families were respected and influential in the area. Sally was a supporter of Tecumseh.

Back in England, William C. Shortt remarried, started an English family and rose in rank. In 1803, he transferred from the Twenty-Fourth Regiment of Foot to the Forty-First. During the War of 1812, he was sent back to Canada, and after almost twenty years, he returned to the Detroit area. It is not known if William and Sally met again, but it is certain that in the small frontier community, she knew he was back.

Lieutenant Colonel William Shortt found himself back in Ohio. After failing to take Fort Meigs on the Maumee River, English General Procter attempted to invade Ohio by means of the Sandusky River. The English fleet sailed up the Sandusky River to the site of current-day Fremont, Ohio, on August 1, 1813. There they encountered a small, crude fort under the command of twenty-one-year-old American Major George Croghan. With only 160 men and one cannon, Croghan was outnumbered eight to one. That night, the English ships bombarded the fort but were unable to breach the walls. Croghan noticed the English were concentrating their fire on one spot in the wall. Betting that this was where they were going to attack, he moved his one cannon to a spot where it could cover the ditch in front of the wall.

On the afternoon of August 2, Lieutenant Colonel William C. Shortt led the first wave in a direct assault on the fort. Covered by smoke from the bombardment, the English got to within fifteen feet of the wall before the Americans saw them and began a rain of small arms fire. Shortt led his men with axes into the ditch, where they began chopping away at the damaged wall. The defenders heard him yell, "Cut away the pickets, my brave boys, and show the damned Yankees no quarter!"[39]

At that point, the Americans opened a porthole that allowed their cannon (nicknamed Old Betsy) to fire directly down into the trench. With one blast of grapeshot, the Americans killed or wounded the entire first wave, including Colonel Shortt. The second wave, charging forward, was unable to stop and fell into the trench on top of their dead and dying comrades. A second blast from Old Betsy destroyed the second wave.

Stunned to see his assault troops destroyed, General Procter decided that the fort could not be taken. He ordered his troops back onboard the ships and sailed back to Detroit, leaving his dead (including Colonel Shortt) behind. Perhaps it's karma, but the man who loved and left Sally Blue Jacket was left—left dead in a ditch.

From Quebec to Wounded Knee by Way of Maumee, Ohio: The Forsyth Family Story

Every day, thousands of motorists cross the Maumee/Perrysburg bridge and pass by an attractive white home on the corner of East Harrison and Conant Street. The two-story house in the Federal style dates to 1826 and was built by Robert Forsyth, Indian agent, trader and the first mayor of Maumee. Almost every local history mentions the house as one of the (if not the) oldest houses in Maumee. There is much more to the story than a pretty old house.

The family who built the house was an integral part of American history. Robert's grandfather fought in one of the most famous battles of the French and Indian War. His aunt married an English officer, who was killed at the Battle of Fallen Timbers. Another aunt was a sister-in-law

The Forsyth House, Maumee, Ohio. *Photo by author.*

to Simon Girty. His uncle was John Kinsie, silversmith, trader and early settler of Chicago, and his father and uncle were Indian agents who fought to protect Indian rights and save white lives during the War of 1812. His first cousin married Juliette Magill (first cousin of Judge James Wolcott of Maumee), who wrote *Wau-Bun*, a best-selling novel of the history of the old Northwest.

Juliette is also the grandmother of Juliette Gordon Low, founder of the American Girl Scouts. Robert, as an Indian agent, oversaw the removal of the last of the Odawa (Ottawa) Indians from Ohio. The Forsyth family history of dealing with Native Americans and Native American issues came to a tragic conclusion in 1890. Robert's nephew James born in Maumee, was in command of the Seventh Calvary Regiment that killed 250 Lakota men, women and children at Wounded Knee, South Dakota.

William and William Jr., 1750–1814

Though the Forsyth name is Scottish, William Forsyth was from Blackwater, Ireland. He arrived in North America around 1750 as part of the English army. Between 1754 and 1763, England and France fought over control of North America in what is often called the French and Indian War. As part of the Sixtieth Regiment of Foot, William fought in several campaigns, including the decisive Siege and Battle of Quebec. In September 1759, English General James Wolfe laid siege to Quebec City on the Saint Lawerence River. The French forces were under the command of Louis-Joseph de Montcalm. Both Wolfe and Montcalm were intelligent and competent commanders. On September 13, the English and French armies met in an open field owned by a farmer named Abraham.

In a brief, one-hour battle, the English were victorious. By a strange fluke, both Wolfe and Montcalm were wounded and died. The story of two heroic generals cut down on the "Plains of Abraham" became an instant legend. The battle decisively doomed French efforts to hang on to North America. It was also the beginning of the end for Native American sovereignty. With the French out of the way, the American colonists looked toward Native lands and began pushing west.

William Forsyth, recovering from two serious wounds received in the battle, began to think of life after the army. When his young wife took ill and died, he was left with four small sons. A surgeon in William's regiment named John Mckenzie also died of a sudden illness, leaving his wife, Emily,

A romantic depiction of the Battle of Quebec: *The Death of Wolfe*, by Benjamin West, 1770. *Courtesy of the National Gallery of Canada, Ottawa.*

alone with two small children. Quicker than you can say, "Let's make a deal," William and Emily were married. They moved to Detroit and opened a tavern just outside the walls of the fort on land he received in exchange for fourteen years of military service. William and Emily raised eight children. His stepson John Kinzie (who, for some reason, dropped the "Mc") and sons Willam Jr., Thomas and Robert became Indian traders. The Forsyth family history is complicated by the family tradition of using the same names in each generation. There is at least one William, James, Robert and Thomas in every generation.

At the time of the American Revolution, Detroit was a small English-held frontier community that had good relations with the Native Americans. Hostages held by the Indians who were ransomed or released often went through Detroit. Two sisters, Eleanor and Margaret Lytle, taken hostage as young children, ended up in Detroit. William Jr. married Margaret. When English Captain Daniel Mckillip died at the battle of Fallen Timbers, his widow, Eleanor Lytle, married John Kinzie. Among the hostages who made their way to Detroit were the Malott family, Sarah and her children. Despite a significant age difference, Sarah's daughter Catherine married the infamous Simon Girty. Her youngest daughter, Keziah, caught eye of

William's brother Thomas, who married her. William Sr. died in 1791, but the complicated role of the Forsyth family in history was just beginning.

As loyalists to the English Crown, the Forsyths and the Kinsies worked closely with the tribes and were respected. After the Battle of Fallen Timbers, one group of Odawa Indians was meeting with Anthony Wayne and preparing to sign the Greenville treaty, while another group was busy signing over land to John Kinsie and Robert Forsyth. These transfers may have been done to prevent the land from falling into American hands. The brothers technically owned vast chunks of the Maumee Valley, the Turkey Foot Creek area in Henry County and everything ("including the islands and both sides of the river") in what is today Farnsworth and Bendview Metroparks. It is believed that John sold his share and used the money to finance his new trade ventures on Lake Michigan.

The War of 1812 brought chaos to the family. John Kinsie and his family were living in Chicago and narrowly escaped death in the Battle of Fort Dearborn. John may be the only man in the war accused of betrayal by the Americans, the Native Americans and the English. Nothing was ever proved. Thomas was the Indian agent in Peoria, Illinois, and a secret agent of the United States. He was almost killed by American rangers who raided his village, burned his home and took him captive. James moved to the Canadian side of the Detroit River and worked for the English. William and Robert survived the fall of Detroit and its reoccupation by the Americans and somehow maintained some neutrality.

In the years after the war, the Forsyth family became invaluable to the U.S. government. They were friends to the Native Americans and did not support Indian removal, but their experience and skills made them part of the process. Robert and James, sons of William Jr. and grandsons of William, the soldier who fought on the Plains of Abraham, now worked as Indian agents.

James and James Jr., 1820–1890

The grass had barely begun to grow on the remains of Fort Miamis and Fort Meigs when the third Forsyth generation arrived in Maumee. In 1826, Robert Forsyth began building his home on a bluff overlooking the Maumee River. Forsyth and John Hunt were partners in a store that traded and sold goods to the Indians and white immigrants. Forsyth's house is believed to have been the first two-story home in Maumee. Forsyth was also an Indian agent and the first mayor of Maumee. Robert's younger brother James also moved to Maumee and probably lived in Robert's house until he married seventeen-year-old Charlotte Templeton Jackson, in Perrysburg. Their first child, James Jr., was born in 1834, in Maumee, possibly in Robert's house.

The Forsyth brothers were shrewd businessmen and made money dealing in land in addition to their other enterprises. James is credited with laying out one of the first lots in Swanton. They were keen on developing the community and keeping their customers happy. Robert and James assisted in the founding of both the Maumee Episcopal Church and the Methodist church.[40]

James and Robert were involved in the 1832 treaty in which the Odawas gave up their remaining lands. Robert received land from the Odawas as he had been extending them credit from his store for years. In the 1830s, the Indian tribes were removed from Ohio and shipped west one by one. Robert was appointed to oversee the removal of the last band of Indians in the Maumee Valley. In the summer of 1839, 108 Odawas boarded a steamship and left Maumee. Robert went with them and used his skills and, sometimes, his money to make sure the Indians received food and shelter. Traveling by steamship, canalboat and overland, the trip to Kansas took the Odawas over a month. Though it was very difficult and the Odawas suffered greatly, only one life was lost. Robert returned to his Maumee home saddened by the removal but proud of the job he had done.[41]

James and Robert continued to prosper in Maumee. In 1851, James Jr. was appointed to West Point. James Sr. continued to work in Indian affairs and was sent west in 1850 to negotiate more treaties. The Civil War was a difficult time for James Sr. In 1864, his brother Robert died at the age of sixty-nine. James had two sons in the Union army. His eldest son, James Jr., was on the staff of Union General Phillip Sheridan. A younger son, George, was a first lieutenant in the 100th Ohio Infantry. George was captured in 1863 and sent to a Confederate prison. On April 13, 1864, he was shot and killed by a guard at Libby Prison in Richmond, Virginia. He is buried in Forest Cemetery in Toledo.

With the third generation of Forsyths passing from the scene and the pioneer era fading, there was still one more scene to be played out in the complicated relationship between the Forsyths and the Indians. James Jr., great-grandson of William, had survived the Civil War and continued his career in the army. On a cold December morning in 1890, Colonel Forsyth surrounded a camp of Lakotas near Wounded Knee Creek, South Dakota. His orders were to disarm them and bring them into the reservation.

Portrait of Civil War Union officers. Left to right: General Philip Sheridan, James Forsyth, Wesley Merrit, Thomas Devin and George A. Custer. *Courtesy of the Medford Historical Society & Museum.*

Something went wrong, a shot was fired and Forsyth's troops, supported by four field pieces, opened up on the almost entirely unarmed camp. An hour later, as many as three hundred Lakota men, women and children lay dead.

The fight was immediately controversial. Forsyth's superior General Nelson A. Miles inspected the battlefield a few days later and was enraged, calling it "the most abominable criminal military blunder and a horrible massacre of women and children."[42] He wanted Forsyth court-martialed and relieved him of duty. The War Department disagreed and reinstated Forsyth. He retired as a general in 1897 and spent his last years in Columbus, Ohio. Forsyth always defended his actions at Wounded Knee. One hundred years later, in 1990, the U.S. Congress officially labeled Wounded Knee a massacre.

It can be said that the Battle of Quebec in 1759 opened the frontier to white settlement. More than 130 years later, in 1890 (the year of Wounded Knee), the U.S. Census Bureau announced that there was no more land available for settlement and proclaimed that the frontier was closed. From the beginning to the end, the Forsyth family was there.

CHAPTER 5

MYTHS, MISCELLANEA AND ENDURING LEGACIES

THE LOST TRIBE OF THE MAUMEE, THE MASCOUTIN

Thanks to James Fenimore Cooper and his famous book *The Last of the Mohicans*, many Americans today will tell you that the Mohicans ceased to exist over two hundred years ago. That is not true. The Mohican tribe suffered horribly and lost their lands, but some managed to survive, and there is a Mohican tribe today. Unlike the Mohicans, some tribes have been lost. The Mascoutin on the Maumee are a people lost in the mists of history.

Following the Battle of Fallen Timbers, Wayne's army burned Indian villages and fields for sixty miles up and down the Maumee. Wayne's soldiers were amazed by the well-kept gardens and miles of cornfields. One area that caught their attention was a large, flat prairie in a wide bend of the Maumee in what is today Henry County. Wayne burned almost four hundred acres of corn in a place he called the Prairie de Masque. *Masque* is French and simply means "mask." Prairie of the Mask sounds odd for a reason. Wayne had it wrong. The real name of the rich bottomland was La Prairie du Mascoutin (Meadow of the Mascoutin). Today, it is a 458-acre state reserve southeast of the town of Liberty Center called the North Turkeyfoot Wildlife Area.

The Mascoutin were a Native American tribe. They were first recorded living in Michigan by Jesuit Missionaries. The name means People of the Little Prairie, though when misspelled the name can also mean "fire," leading some to falsely call them the Fire People. Little is known about them other than that they seem to have been on the losing side in several

Painted wood block depicting the Battle of Fallen Timbers. *Bridgeman Images.*

wars. The French claim that the Mascoutin were one of the largest tribes in the Great Lakes before tribal warfare decimated them in the 1600s. For reasons unknown, they moved south, into the Ohio and the Indiana area. In 1742, one band, allied with the Kickapoo, petitioned the French monarchy to allow them to set up a village on both sides of a broad stretch of the Maumee. For a while, the village seemed to prosper. The fertile bottomland grew plentiful corn. The area was rich in deer, beaver and other valuable fur-bearing animals.

During the French and Indian War (1754–63), the Mascoutin supported the French. Following Pontiac's war and a smallpox outbreak in 1764, the Mascoutin on the Maumee seem to fade out of sight.

Members of the tribe appeared elsewhere in the Midwest. When the American Revolution broke out, many of the Mascoutin were living with the Miami and the Wea on the Wabash River. They attempted to remain neutral. American General George Rogers Clark put an end to their

The Fallen Timbers Battlefield Monument. *Photo by author.*

The Meadow of the Mascoutin, a bottomland along the Maumee River. *Photo by author.*

neutrality by attacking and burning villages on the Wabash River. White aggression did not end with the end of the revolution. It is believed that there were Mascoutin living with Kickapoo when Kentucky militia destroyed the villages of Ouiatenon in 1791. There is a tradition of Mascoutin people living in Wisconsin, and there is a town in Illinois named after them. The last mention of the Mascoutin in American records is in 1825, when a few survivors are mentioned living with the Kickapoo Prairie band. Then the records go silent, and the Mascoutin disappear.

It is possible that some Mascoutin may yet come forward, and there may still exist an oral record of their culture and traditions. But if so, they have flown under the white radar for two hundred years.

As for the once prosperous village on the Maumee, it is now a wooded wildlife area named after Ottawa Chief Turkey Foot, who may never have existed. Oddly, the original name has survived, in a sense. Early American settlers struggled to make sense of the French name. Eventually they changed it to a biblical name they were familiar with, and Du Mascoutin became Damascus. Today the area is Damascus Township in Henry County. State Route 109 crosses the Maumee on the Damascus Bridge. If you have reason to cross that bridge, there is a fine view to the east of "La Prairie du Mascoutin."

The Ghost Ride of General Anthony Wayne

According to legend, every January 1 (the birthday of Major General Anthony Wayne), his ghost rises from his first grave in Erie, Pennsylvania, and rides across almost the entire state to his second grave in the family cemetery in Radnor.

Erie, Pennsylvania, was a remote military outpost in 1796. When Wayne unexpectedly died there, he was buried by the flagpole. Thirteen years later, in 1809, his son arrived in Erie to exhume his father and bring his bones back to the family plot in Radnor. With the exception of his left leg, Wayne's body was almost perfectly preserved, which caused a problem. Isaac Wayne had made the journey on rough roads in a small carriage with no room for a full-size decaying corpse.

A local surgeon came up with a solution. Wayne's body was cut into small sections and boiled in a rendering pot. His clean bones were then packed for the journey home. The liquid remains were buried, along with the knives used to dismember him, near the blockhouse. In a macabre

"Erie's famous Wayne pot." *Erie County Historical Museum. Photo by author.*

side note, Wayne's right boot was in such good condition that a local tavern owner named Duncan kept it and had a match made.[43] Wayne was known to have spent some quality time in taverns. It seems fitting that his boots continued to spend time in a tavern long after he was gone.

Wayne's son placed his remains in a basket and took them home. After the four-hundred-mile journey, he discovered that some of the general's bones were missing. Apparently, they bounced out and were lost along the way. The legend says that at midnight on January 1, Anthony Wayne rises from the ground near the Erie Blockhouse on a black ghost horse and rides across the state of Pennsylvania looking for his lost bones. Of course, it's just a story, but if you're in Pennsylvania on January 1 you might want to avoid US Route 322. Just saying.

THE LEGEND OF TURKEY FOOT ROCK

Turkey Foot rock has teased and taunted historians for two hundred years, and the truth behind the legend still evades us.

As a boy, in the 1820s, Dresden Howard attended a mission school on the east bank of the Maumee. Many of his classmates were Odawa (Ottawa) Indians. Dresden learned many of their stories, and writing years later, he recorded the story of a chief named Turkey Foot, who stood on a rock to rally his warriors and was shot down. Dresden does not specify where the rock was.

A poem about the Fallen Timbers titled "The Forest Rangers" was written by Andrew Coffinberry and published in 1842. Coffinberry refers to the chief as "Brave Me-sa-sa" and places him dying upon "a large rough stone" at the foot of Presque Isle. On a fall day in 1860, Peter Navarre, the famed local frontiersman, gave the historian and artist Benson Lossing a tour of the ruins of Fort Meigs, Fort Miamis and the area where it was believed the Battle of Fallen Timbers was fought. Sitting along the river between Maumee and Waterville, Lossing did a quick drawing of Turkey Foot Rock while Navarre

Turkey-Foot's Rock, by Benson Lossing, 1860. Lossing would do rough drawings in the field and finish them later, leading to some mistakes. *From Benson Lossing's* Pictorial Field-book of the War of 1812.

told him the story of Chief Turkey Foot, or Me-sa-sa. Navarre's version combines elements of Coffinberry's poem and Dresden's story. According to Navarre, at the height of the battle, the chief jumped up onto the rock, at which point a bullet found him and he fell dead. Navarre stated that he witnessed Native Americans stopping at the rock to leave offerings and to mourn the loss of the great leader. In this version, the bird feet were carved into the rock to honor the chief.[44]

Benson Lossing's *Pictorial Field-book of the War of 1812* (published 1868) made the rock part of American history—for a while, at least. Turkey Foot Rock became a famous local attraction visited by presidents, celebrities and vandals. Over time, the stories became more elaborate and far-fetched. In one version, the dying chief takes his tomahawk and, with his last breath, carves his symbolic name, Turkey Foot, into the rock. Another version ties the rock to the battle but not to any individual. Cutting Marsh was a missionary on the Maumee. On February 14, 1830, Marsh wrote in his diary,

> *There is a large stone at the foot of Presque Isle having the print of a turkey, rabbits and also of a horse's foot on it. On this rock the Indians imagined some spirit who was angry with them, came and stood, during the battle, in the form of a turkey, accordingly almost to the present time they offer a sacrifice of whiskey and tobacco on the rock whenever they pass it.*

Bird spirits are common in many traditional Native American belief systems. If the petroglyphs on the rock represent a spirit, they could predate the actual battle of Fallen Timbers. Perhaps they represent a spirit who turned against the Natives the day of the battle, or they could even be a tribute to Nimkii, the Thunderbird. In the mythology of many tribes, including the Odawa, the Thunderbird is a giant and very powerful being. Seeking the protection of Nimkii would seem to be a wise thing to do at a river crossing. Nimkii, it is said, often fought with Mishibizhii, a spirit who lived underwater and liked to drown people.

For an inanimate object, the rock has inspired a lot of controversy. It became a popular Victorian tourist attraction. Vandals enhanced the existing bird's feet and added more. In 1899, history enthusiasts from Toledo, planning the Ohio's 1903 centennial celebration, thought the rock would be a nice part of the festivities and stole it. Angry Maumee residents, led by Mayor Daniel Cooke, demanded it back. The Toledo Centennial failed to get funding, and one night, the rock was dumped back in Maumee. The people of Maumee

Turkey Foot Rock, River Road and the spa in the 1916 flood. The sign says, "Open for business." *Photo courtesy of the Lucas County Library.*

A family outing at Turkey Foot Rock. *Courtesy of the Lucas County Library.*

threw a party celebrating its return. It was called a "public jollification," which sounds like a lot more fun than a "Centennial Commemoration."

The rock was returned to its spot along River Road, an iron fence was built around it and it continued to be a local attraction. In 1953, it was moved from its location on River Road to a spot of honor next to the Fallen Timbers Monument. The Ohio History Connection (known at the time as the Ohio Historical Society) saw the rock as an appropriate monument to the Native American role in the battle of Fallen Timbers, and it still plays a part in remembrances and ceremonies. Offerings of tobacco are still left at the site, and Native Americans still visit the rock.

The true meaning of Turkey Foot Rock may never be known. What we do know is that the original carvings were almost certainly done by Native Americans. The rock was located at a popular fording spot on the river. The rock was not on the Fallen Timbers battlefield, but that does not mean it was not a tribute to the battle or to the fallen. Contrary to what I have been saying for years, Turkey Foot is an Odawa name, but there is no record of a Chief Turkey Foot. There was a great Odawa chief who led his warriors at the Battle of Fallen Timbers and fell, severely wounded, at the height of the battle. It is possible that this Odawa chief, Egushawa, was the real Turkey Foot, but he never stood on this rock. Dr. Michael Pratt's archaeology and subsequent studies indicate that this rock was not actually located on the

Top: Turkey Foot Rock, Victorian tourist attraction. Unknown child, circa 1900. *Courtesy of the Lucas County Library.*

Bottom: Unknown children, circa 1900. *Courtesy of the Lucas County Library.*

battlefield. There is also the minor issue that it is upside down. Jim Murphy, a retired Ohio State University librarian with a Master of Science degree in geology from Case Western Reserve University, did a study and discovered that sometime between 1931 and 1953, the rock got flipped; it is currently resting upside down.

While it is tempting to dismiss the legend of Turkey Foot Rock as a myth, it has become part of the battle story. There is no great man-made or natural feature that distinguishes the Fallen Timbers Battlefield. There was never a ruined chapel or rugged hilltop around which to tell the story.

We don't even have a cemetery where we can remember the dead. What we do have is a mysterious carved rock which, for a long time, was the only symbol of Fallen Timbers. Offerings on the rock are made not to remember a fallen individual but to remember all the fallen. Until the monument was built in 1929, there was no reminder, no memorial, no trace of the battle except for Turkey Foot Rock. The memory of Fallen Timbers has been preserved by a rock, and that makes it a very special rock and a real part of our history.

Turkey Foot Rock today, at its location near the Fallen Timbers Battlefield Monument. Compared to earlier photos, it does appear to be upside down. *Photo by author.*

A House of Ill Repute and a Blackwater Spring

Turkey Foot Rock, now located at the Fallen Timbers Memorial, was originally located on the north side of River Road just west of Jerome Road. On the other side of River Road, literally on the banks of the Maumee, was a strange two-story building. Over the years, it was home to several businesses and known by many names. In a way, it was the first Fallen Timbers visitor's center, but it was never a business that made the town fathers proud. I sincerely hope I do not slander someone's ancestors by retelling this story, and I apologize if anyone is offended.

The establishment known as the Spa was built near Turkey Foot Rock. Early history tourists would stop there for food and or refreshments. The owners took advantage of a foul-smelling sulfur spring next to the rock and claimed that drinking the water was good for your health. They based this on "old Indian wisdom." Probably the only medicinal value in the water was its ability to purge the body. Old-timers claim that, usually within fifteen to thirty minutes of drinking the stuff, the consumer would experience explosive diarrhea. Modern science has confirmed that high levels of sulfur in drinking water does cause diarrhea. So, in reality, the spa was a place to go and get your insides cleaned out.

This fact was apparently unknown to President Rutherford B. Hayes. In 1888, the then former president was part of a delegation of prominent officials who were inspecting Ohio battle sites. Their goal, officially, was to see what could be done to save these historic locations. Unofficially, the group, which included Ohio Governor Joseph Foraker, met with and promoted local Republican politicians. On the morning of August 14, the group stopped to inspect Turkey Foot Rock and the supposed site of the Battle of Fallen Timbers. They then paused at the sulfur spring.

At this point, Hayes had a truly presidential "hold my beer" moment. Waxing nostalgic about his days as a young lawyer, Hayes recalled trying cases in Maumee. In a display of manliness, Hayes drank heartily from the spring while the others and even the horses "made wry faces." Despite the awful smell, several in the party managed to swallow some of the very foul water.[45] The party then boarded their carriages and proceed to Maumee and a lunch in Perrysburg. History does not record what happened next, but it is a good bet that they did not get far before the explosive diarrhea kicked in. A president, a governor and several prominent politicians running for the bushes was not exactly material for a Currier & Ives print.

As late as 1896, the health benefits of the spring were still being promoted. In the early twentieth century, however, the reputation of the house took another turn. The spa, outside the legal jurisdiction of either Maumee or Waterville, became a roadhouse and a hot party spot. Allegedly, it was, at one point, even a brothel. With the advent of Prohibition, you could also get illegal booze there. Like many such establishments, it did not prosper once Prohibition was repealed. The last role played by the spa was that of a restaurant in the 1940s and early 1950s known as the Stagecoach Inn. Its specialty was fried chicken made with chickens raised on-site. The building was torn down in the 1950s. The rock was moved in 1953, and the spring no longer exists. In the winter, when the foliage dies on the bank of the Maumee, the foundations of the building are still visible.

It is human nature to think that our ancestors were more upright and lawful than current generations, but when the nearest visitor's center to a national historic site offers moonshine, loose women and fried chicken, the premise is debatable.

The Myth of the Warriors at the Gate

For two hundred years, every account of the Battle of Fallen Timbers has told the story of the Native Americans fleeing to Fort Miamis and seeking protection only to find that the English had closed the gates and would not let them in. Blue Jacket and Tecumseh at the gate angrily cursing the British commander makes for an unforgettable image. Problem is, it almost certainly didn't happen. While the Brits did lead the Native Americans to believe that they would support them and fight with them, they did not, and the Native confederacy was enraged and felt betrayed. The Indians had expected the English to engage with Wayne's army, and when that did not happen, they were bitterly disappointed. Tecumseh and other Native leaders would state for years that the British had closed the door in their face and "barred the gate against the poor Indians."

In truth, the barring of the gate was more of a metaphor than an actual event. It is unlikely any Indians sought shelter in the fort. Forting up was not a popular style of fighting among Native Americans, as they preferred tactics suited to the woods and open meadows. Secondly, Fort Miamis was a small, crowded structure, and half the garrison was suffering from malaria. It was not an appealing place. The legend also ignores the fact that there was not room in the fort for the number of warriors on the field that day. It is also worth noting that many, if not most, of the warriors had family camped in the Swan Creek area, now downtown Toledo. Taking shelter in Fort Miamis would have left their families unprotected.

Lastly, if any Indians had wanted to enter the fort, they would probably have found it impossible. On the morning of August 20, 1794, Major Campbell, commander of Fort Miamis, heard gunfire in the distance from the battle. Around eleven o'clock, Campbell noticed Indians streaming through the woods in front of the fort. He had orders to not engage the Americans unless forced to. Therefore, he did what any commander of an outpost in a foreign land facing an unknown threat would do: he locked down the fort. Gaps in the abatis (rows of sharp, pointed logs placed around the earthworks) were filled. Piles of thorny brush were rolled into the ditches around the fort. The chevaux-de-frise (rolls of wooden spikes) were put in place, and some were, no doubt, placed in front of the gate. Every man was at his combat post. Every gun and field piece was primed and loaded. This is not a situation that invites people to knock at the door.

The only record we have of anyone entering or attempting to enter the fort on the day of the battle refers to Indian agent Alexander McKee. McKee came in late in the day after Wayne had made camp, and he came in from the river in a canoe.

So the story of angry Indians banging on a barred gate probably never happened. Still, the sense of betrayal was very real. The total failure of the English to assist the Native cause in any way at Fallen Timbers may have done more to discourage Indian resistance than the actual battle. It was a

Fort Miamis. On the day of the battle, these ditches would have been filled with pointed logs, thorn bushes and chevaux-de-frise. *Photo by author.*

Chevaux-de-frise. *Photo by author.*

point Tecumseh would bring up in negotiations with British for the rest of his life. While the British did not literally bar the gate to poor Indians fleeing the Americans, in a sense, they did. That snub may have cost them the entire Old Northwest.

The Weapons of 1794

An Easy Guide to Eighteenth-Century Military Muskets

During the 1700s, England and France fought all over the world, including in what is now the United States. The French-made Charleville and the English Brown Bess were the M16 and AK-47 of the day. Some Canadians, Indians and probably American militia were carrying the Brown Bess at Fallen Timbers. The Charleville was the weapon carried by the United States infantry. A shorter version was carried by the dragoons (cavalry).

Both weapons were improved and revised for over one hundred years, so there are many varieties and special versions of each rifle in existence.

The basics: the Charleville is longer but lighter and lower caliber. Both were fitted with a triangular bayonet. The Bess in the photo is fitted with a flash guard and frizzen cover for safety. Neither would have likely been on an original.

At a glance, the expert will notice the differences in lock design and stock. The easiest and quickest way to tell the difference is the barrel bands. The Charleville has two; Bess has none. The Bess does have a swell in the stock for your left hand. In other words, Bess has more curves, but Madame Charleville has a wedding band (two, actually).

Charleville
1717–1840
7,721,000 made
Caliber: .69
Height: 60 inches,
Barrel: 45 inches
Weight: 10 pounds

Brown Bess
1722–1838
4,300,000 made
Caliber: .75
Height: 58.5 inches
Barrel: 42 inches
Weight: 10.5 pounds

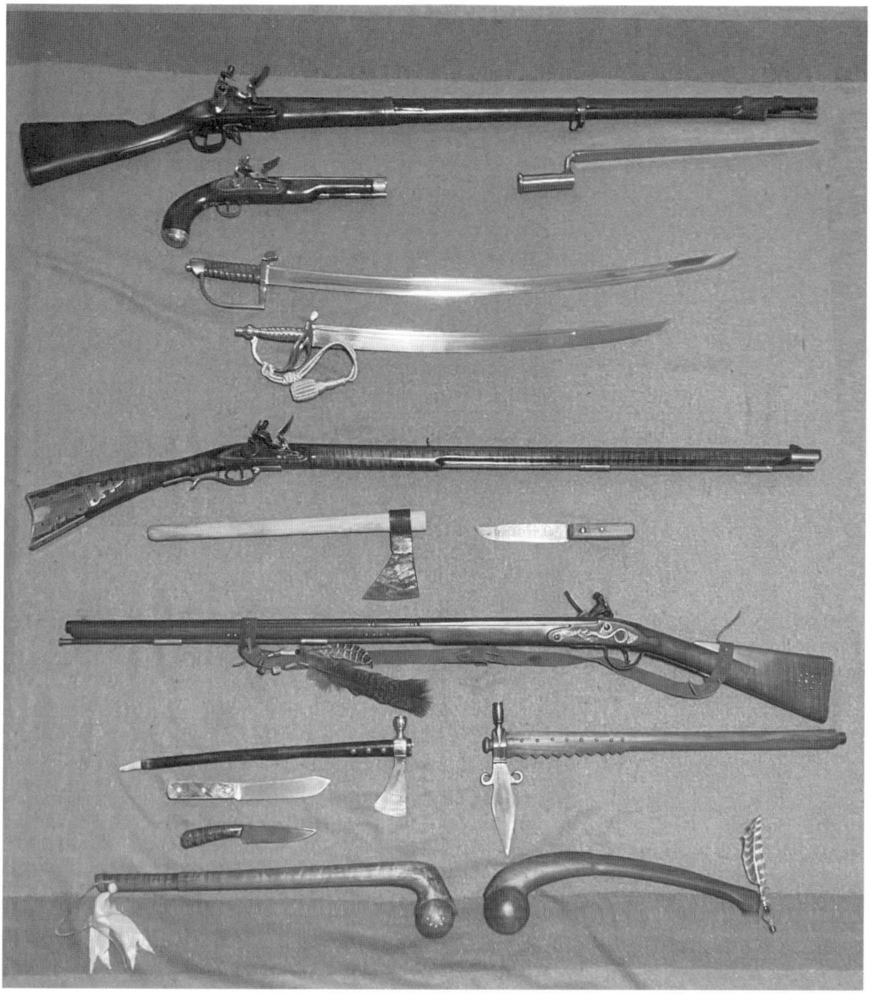

Weapons of Fallen Timbers. *Author's collection.*

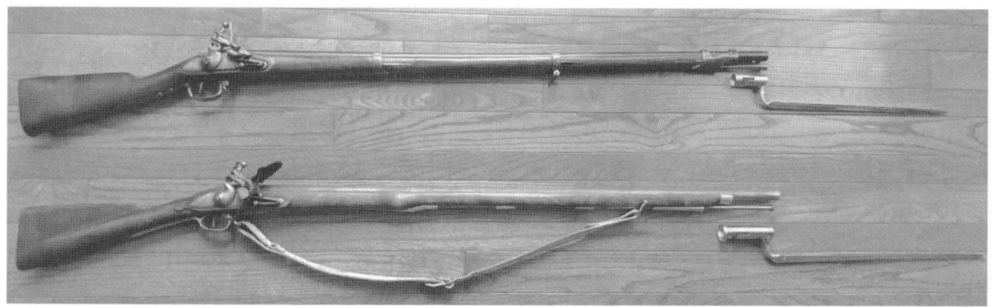

The Charleville musket (*top*) and the Brown Bess (*bottom*): the M16 and AK-47 of 1794. *Author's collection.*

Why Is the British Land Pattern Musket Called the Brown Bess?

First commissioned in 1722, the British Land Pattern Musket, with some updates, saw action on every continent for over a century. As these muskets were the official long arm of the British army and popular with colonists, there is no doubt they were present at the Battle of Fallen Timbers. This musket played a huge part in American history, appearing in the French and Indian War, the American Revolution and the War of 1812. It was the British musket used during the Napoleonic Wars, as well as in the colonial wars in India, Africa and Asia. Though officially replaced in 1838, the British Land Pattern Musket continued to show up. Mexican General Santa Anna's army was equipped with it when they took the Alamo. One was even found on the American Civil War battlefield at Shiloh. It is believed that it was the weapon of a Confederate soldier who was wounded or killed.

So where did the nickname Brown Bess come from? We don't know, but there are plenty of theories. It has been said that the musket was named after an earlier weapon called the Brown Bill. There is no connection between the weapons, though, so most experts say no. Some say it was named for the anti-rust compound the army issued to preserve the barrel. However, this compound was not issued until 1808, and the name was in use at least fifty years earlier, so that is another no. Some have claimed it is a corruption of the word *arquebus*, which was a much older weapon. The word *arquebus*, though, was out of common usage when the gun was made, so that's also a no. Another theory is that the name comes from the German *braun büchse*, or brown gun. But experts say that is also highly unlikely. Some say it was called brown because the barrel rusted. This, though, is another no because the English army did not like rusty barrels. In fact, not maintaining your weapon could get you severely flogged. Perhaps it was named after Queen Elizabeth of England? Yes and no. Elizabeth had died over one hundred years earlier, but she was very popular, making Elizabeth the most common name for girls at the time. As a name, Elizabeth would have been reserved for the aristocrats and the wealthy. Most common, lower-class or, as we would say, "normal" girls would have been Bess. Nothing unusual about a soldier giving his weapon a female name. They were very close.

English soldier John Shipp wrote about the soldier and his musket:

> *It is his best and dearest friend in time of need; his pillow on which he rests his weary head; it is his constant companion day and night; it defends*

British army officer and soldier with a Brown Bess, late eighteenth century. From *George B. Campion's* History of the Corps of Royal Sappers and Miners, *vol. 1.*

> *his name and honor against the encroachment of his enemies; it is his dependance; it warms his cold chilly bosom; he is wedded to it in honor—bound to it by love—riveted to it by long tried attachment. It is his great and sure peace-maker between him and his foes; they seldom quarrel, save when she misses fire, but which is not intentional, but from the cold damps of night, and the silvery dews of morn, or the drenching rain. It is more—it is his shield that will ward off the impending blow of his foe.*

But where did the "brown" part come from? I think it was simply a reflection of the class realities and social fashions of the day. Life in preindustrial Britain was largely conducted outdoors. The lower on the English social scale you were, the more time you spent outside. On the other hand, the wealthier you were, the less sun you saw, and pale white skin was proof of it. Aristocratic ladies took great pains to avoid the sun and used makeup and powder to show how elite they were. Women of the middle and lower classes could not avoid the sun, so they tanned, burned or freckled. It stands to reason that the object of a British soldier's heart was not some milky white Elizabeth pining away in a castle but a strong and lovely brown Bess.

Mishebeshu: The Monster on the Musket

Books, TV and movies until recently portrayed frontier warfare as including a hero in a coonskin cap with a trusty long rifle, holding his ground as arrows rained down around him. The truth looked a lot different. Bows and arrows were still popular with Indians at this time for hunting but not in war. While bows and arrows were cheap and easy to make, they were not relied on in battle. By the late 1700s, metal points had replaced flint arrowheads. Dr. Pratt's archaeological survey of the Fallen Timbers Battlefield in 1995 did turn up some prehistoric flint pieces, but no metal arrowheads were recovered. Both that and a later 2001 survey found more than six hundred lead projectiles (musket balls, rifle balls and shot).

The Indians at Fallen Timbers used firearms, and the most popular firearm was the Northwest Trade Gun, also known as the fusil.[46] This large-caliber smoothbore gun was produced in England. It ranged in quality from dangerously inexpensive to the elaborate "chief's gun." Trade guns were very versatile. They could be loaded with light buckshot for small game or heavy shot and ball for big game or war. They were the most widely used guns on the frontier. Their distinguishing characteristics are a large trigger guard, a barrel that starts octagonal at the stock and becomes round and a sea serpent or dragon on the left side.

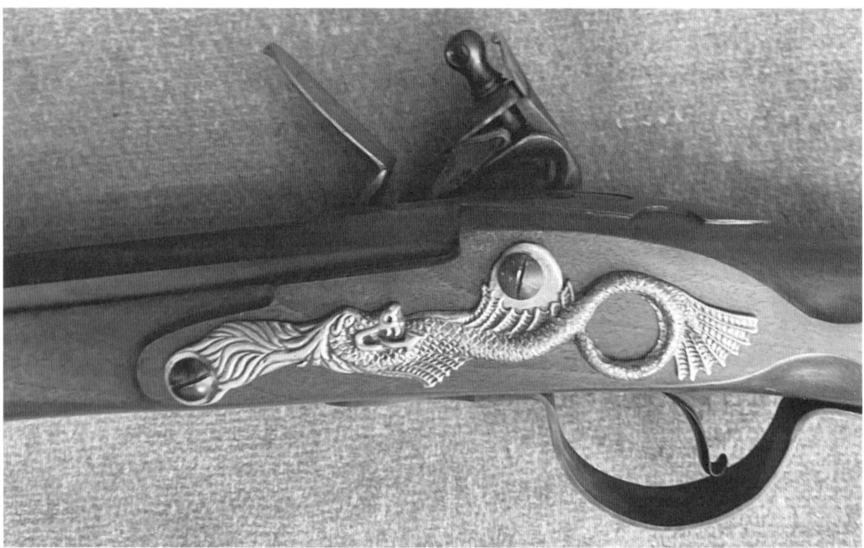

Trade gun replica. *Author's collection.*

These guns were produced from the 1740s into the early twentieth century and were used everywhere. Every Native leader, from Pontiac to Sitting Bull, had one. The Museum of the Fur Trade in Chadron, Nebraska, has one believed to have been owned by Tecumseh. They were mass-produced for the Indian trade, and quality was often sacrificed in favor of profit. Shortly before the Battle of Fallen Timbers, Indian agent Alexander McKee bitterly complained about a shipment he received at his trading post on the Maumee. The English had shipped him junk guns that tended to explode when fired.

So while the well-made and highly accurate Pennsylvania long rifle has become the glamor girl of history, its hardworking Native counterpart has almost been forgotten. The most distinguishing feature of the trade gun is also the most likely to be misinterpreted. The brass figure of the sea serpent on the left side was present on almost every trade gun produced. Flawed explanations I've read include it being a fire-breathing dragon since guns shoot fire. Another common explanation is that Indians thought bullets were poison, like the venom of a snake. That is sort of silly, though it is amusing

Agawa Bay pictographs, Ontario. *Photo by author.*

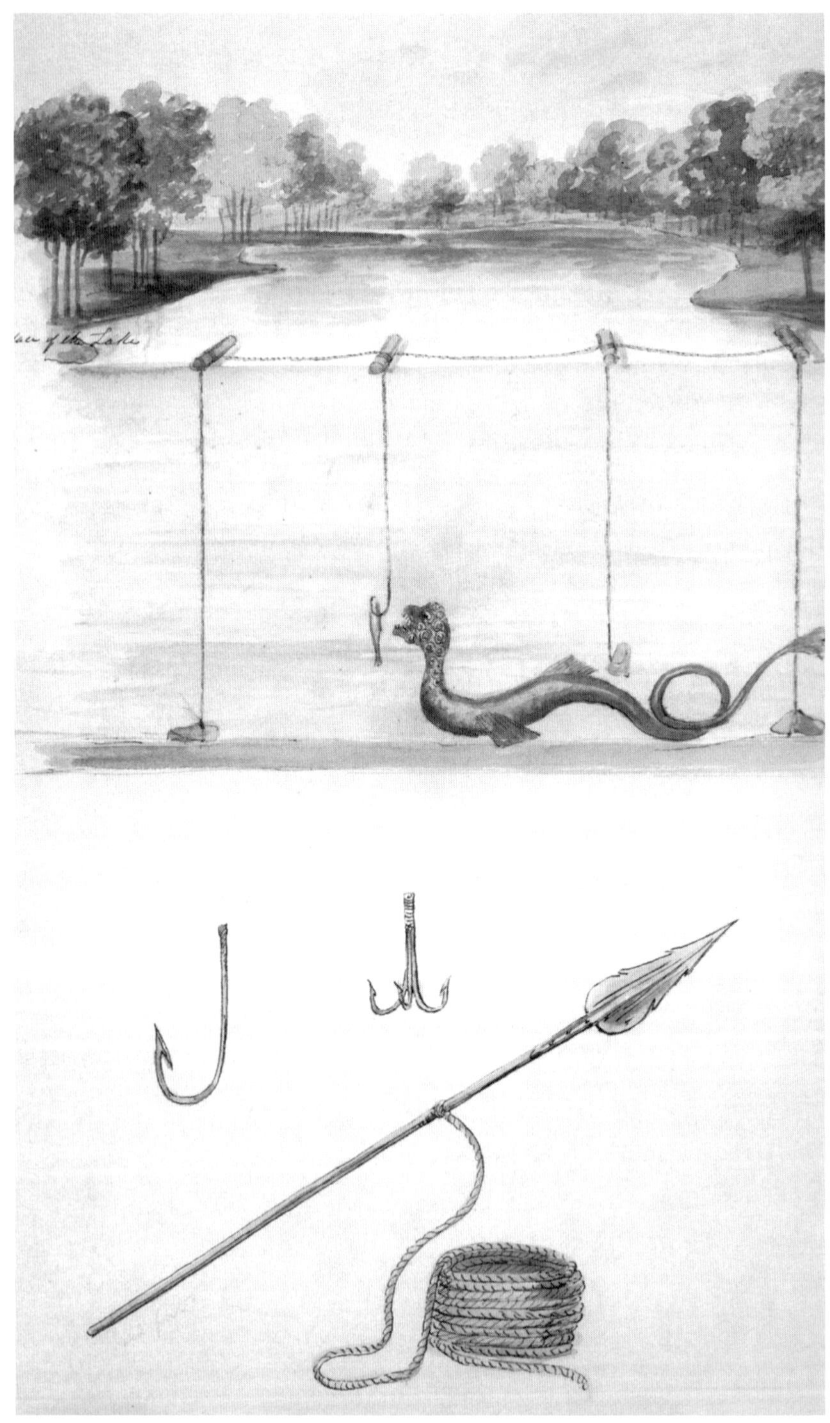
of the Lake

Opposite: *Trapping Lake Monster*, George Winter, circa 1835. *From* Indians and a Changing Frontier: The Art of George Winters, *published by the Indian Historical Society, 1993.*

Above: Trade gun. *Author's collection.*

to think that maybe Native Americans understood lead was poisonous one hundred years before white scientists did.

The truth may lie in the stories of the Great Lakes people. The sea serpent may represent Mishebeshu (or Mishipizeh), the great underwater panther who lived in the depths of lakes and rivers. He had the body of a panther as well as scales, horns on his head and a long tail. Mishebeshu was a killer and could assist you in hunting or in war; it was said that if you traveled across rivers and lakes, it was wise to have his blessing, or he might drown you. When angry, he could create great storms. Though the details vary, the great lake monster appears in the stories of almost every Native American tribal group literally from the Yucatan to the Yukon. He appears, with horns, in a pictograph on the shores of Lake Superior. He appears in a painting by George Winter in southern Indiana. He appears on a trade gun owned by Lakota holy man Sitting Bull.

The brass Mishebeshu is said to bring good luck. Canadian archaeologists studying village sites have found many intentionally broken brass Mishebeshus. They believe that when a gun wore out or was broken beyond repair, the owner would pry Mishebeshu off and break the figure before discarding it because the luck was gone.[47]

Luck was not with the Indians at the Battle of Fallen Timbers. In the debris of battle, there were no doubt many trade guns lost. Leaves fell; the forest grew; the guns were buried. It is very possible that somewhere in modern-day Maumee, a brass representation of the great horned underwater panther lies sleeping. It's probably best we don't disturb him.

Fallen Timbers and U.S. Army Rifle No. 1

Among the items found in the archaeological survey of the Fallen Timbers Battlefield in 1995 were a few pieces of a flintlock rifle. Many assume that it belonged to a Native American or a Kentucky militiaman. A third possibility is that it belonged to a member of a regular army rifle brigade. If that could be proven, these few pieces might represent one of the first U.S. army rifles ever made.

During the American Revolution and for the first years of the republic, our military was armed with muskets made in England and France and privately owned hunting rifles. That changed after the disastrous defeat of Arthur St. Clair's army in 1791. As part of the effort to build a professional army, the government contracted with several Pennsylvania gunmakers to produce an American rifle for the newly organized rifle brigades. The 1792 Contract rifle was the first firearm made specifically for the U.S. Army. As U.S. Army rifle no. 1, you would assume the 1792 would be one of the most famous firearms in history. Oddly, it is little known and surrounded by controversy and myth.

Its origins are straightforward enough. Secretary of War Henry Knox appointed Revolutionary War General Edward Hand to develop a functional military rifle. After studying the problem, meeting with gunsmiths and having prototypes tested, they agreed on a .49-caliber, maple stocked long rifle with a patch box in the stock and a forty-two-inch barrel. Eleven gunsmiths made 1,476 rifles by the end of 1792. In 1794, another 2,000 were made. That is about the last point historians agree on.

Today, there are no proven examples of this gun in existence. Part of the problem is its design: 1792 contract rifles looked like civilian long rifles, did not

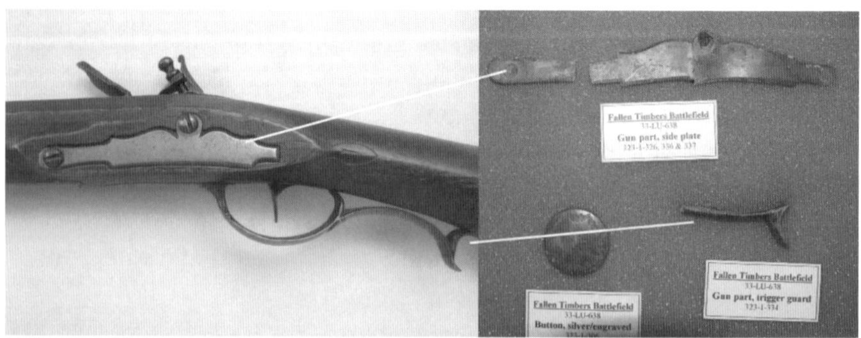

A flintlock rifle made by Jacob Dickert and rifle parts found on the Fallen Timbers Battlefield. *American-Firearms.com and author's photo.*

have sling swivels or bayonet mounts and may not have even been stamped "U.S." The lack of military markings and features makes it difficult to tell if a rifle is a 1792 contract or one of thousands of hunting rifles made and sold to the public. This also made 1792 contracts easy to steal, which may be what happened to many of them. The topic is also complicated by the legend of the American rifleman versus the musket-wielding infantryman. Muskets of the day were mass-produced and inaccurate. However, they were three times quicker to reload and were equipped with a bayonet. Rifles were more than three times as accurate but slow to reload, difficult to maintain and useless against bayonets. In the hands of skilled marksmen, the Pennsylvania long rifle was deadly. In the hands of untrained troops, it was a disaster.

Though the rifleman is glamorized in fiction and American literature, serious historians often downplay his role. This controversy in American history may have led to the role of the 1792 rifle and Wayne's riflemen being downplayed or ignored.

There is not even agreement on what the rifles were used for. Some historians have stated the rifles were low quality and produced as giveaways for Indians. There are some problems with the junk gun position. Some rifles may have been used in negotiations with Native people, and with many different gunsmiths involved, some of the weapons were undoubtedly inferior. However, most of the gunmakers involved were the best of the day, including Jacob Dickert. Dickert was born in Germany and immigrated to Pennsylvania as a young man. His rifles were used during the American Revolution, the War of 1812 and long after his death. One of his rifles was found in the Alamo and is currently on display in the Alamo Museum.

Not all the guns, if any, were given away. In 1803, Meriwether Lewis visited the U.S. armory at Harpers Ferry and reported it still had three hundred of these rifles in storage. He took fifteen on his famous expedition.

We also know that by the end of 1792, several hundred of these guns had been shipped to Pittsburgh and, presumably, downriver to where Wayne's Legion was training.[48]

So are the few pieces found on the Fallen Timbers Battlefield from America's first army rifle? Gunsmith and historian Alan Gutchess believes that the debris found is not from a 1792 rifle, based on its measurements, though he says it is in fact in the style of a Dickert/Lancaster rifle.

There is a strong argument in favor of the gun being a 1792 contract. These rifles were all made individually by different gunsmiths, so their size would not have been uniform. The debris was found in an area where a rifle company was deployed. There are also similarities between

Militiamen with long rifles at a reenactment of the Battle of Fallen Timbers. *Photo by author.*

the side plate and guns built by the same makers. With just a few broken pieces to go on, we may never know if this is really a 1792 contract rifle. Still, it is amazing to think that a rifle found in Maumee, Ohio; the rifles used by Lewis and Clark; and a rifle found in the smoking ruins of the Alamo are all related and may even have been made by the same hands in the same shop.

ANTHONY WAYNE AND FALLEN TIMBERS IN POPULAR CULTURE

The Earliest Known European Painting of an Ohio Landscape Was Created in Perrysburg

Early Ohio history is often illustrated with paintings of lush landscapes. Most people would assume that the first painting done by a white person in Ohio would be a scene of the Ohio River or the rolling hills of eastern Ohio. Christopher Busta-Peck, Cleveland librarian and historian, has researched close to three thousand paintings done in Ohio prior to the Civil War. He

Wayne in popular culture. *Photo by author.*

thinks the earliest landscape painted in Ohio was a view of the Maumee River done in what is now Perrysburg, Ohio.

When Anthony Wayne began moving north from Cincinnati in 1793, the English governor of Lower Canada, John Simcoe, came to Ohio and authorized the construction of Fort Miamis in current-day Maumee.

View on the Miami River, by Elizabeth Simcoe, 1794. *Courtesy of the British Library.*

Lieutenant Robert Pilkington was the engineer assigned to build Fort Miamis. He was also an artist. In March 1794, he painted an image of the Maumee, which he called the Miamis River. In the right foreground is Alexander McKee's trading post near what is today Riverside Park in Perrysburg. To the left is Audubon Island with a cabin on it. The center of the picture is the site of Fort Miamis in Maumee. The boat in front of McKee's post is flying the British Union Jack.

This watercolor is currently in the Ontario provincial archives. Pilkington was a close friend of Elizabeth Simcoe, the governor's wife. Elizabeth Simcoe later, in 1794, painted a copy of the landscape at Fort York, current-day Toronto. Simcoe's painting is the better-known one, having appeared in Elizabeth Simcoe's book and diary of her life on the Canadian frontier. Simcoe's painting currently resides in the British Library. Elizabeth Simcoe was never in Ohio, so her painting is based on Pilkington's descriptions and a little imagination. In the center of her painting, we see Fort Miamis under construction.

Miamis River (Maumee), by Robert Pilkington, 1774. *Courtesy of the Ontario provincial archives.*

Approximately the same location as Robert Pilkington's watercolor today. *Photo by author.*

Anthony Wayne, Rock Star

Anthony Wayne was only fifty-one years old when he died. He was at the height of his popularity, fame and power. He was a national hero in an era where military heroes dominated popular culture. They were the movie star/rock star idols of the day. Their adventures were followed in the popular press and their lives gossiped about. They wore glittering uniforms, rode the best horses and drank the best wine. They were America's idols. Wayne lived in a time where it was possible to be both Napoleon and Elvis, George Armstrong Custer and Lady Gaga.

His victory at Fallen Timbers electrified the American public and captured the popular imagination. Warfare between the New Americans and the Native Americans was horrible and brutal. The situation before Fallen Timbers was grim. Then Wayne moved an army over two hundred miles into the wilderness and successfully engaged and destroyed a large enemy force while humiliating the hated English at Fort Miamis.

Wayne achieved instant pop star hero status for this. He was aware of the value of projecting a good PR image. His nickname, Mad Anthony Wayne, was no accident. He was a stern disciplinarian and a meticulous planner while appearing to be a rash, impulsive risk-taker. Wayne once told George Washington, "If you give the command, I'll storm hell!" Great media line.

Wayne even had a rock star girlfriend. He was always a womanizer, but once his wife died in 1790, he went public. Mary Vining was eleven years younger and reputedly the most beautiful woman in the colonies. Born to a wealthy family, she led a glamorous life of fashion, parties and romance. During the American Revolution, British and American officers alike courted her, and many proposed marriage. The only picture we have of her is a drawing done by British Major John Andre, who adored her. Andre was caught acting as a spy for Benedict Arnold and executed. After the success of the Fallen Timbers campaign and the Greenville Treaty, Wayne returned to Philadelphia. He made the social rounds of dinners, parties and even the theater with the lovely

Mary Vining, by Major John Andre. *From* Colonial Homesteads and Their Stories, *by Marion Harland & the Ridgely Family.*

Miss Vining on his arm. After his unexpected death in 1796, Mary went into seclusion and wore black the rest of her life.

Of course, stars eventually lose their shine. While Wayne remains a star in the history books, he has faded from the public awareness. But unlike rock stars, Wayne is remembered by counties, cities, schools, rivers and bridges.

To this day, there are more places in the United States named for Wayne than for any non-president. There are Wayne Counties in fifteen states. Nine cities are named Wayne. There are six Waynesboros, two Waynesvilles and two Waynesburgs, as well as Wayne City, Waynetown, Fort Wayne, Waynes Trace, Wayne Heights and Anthony Wayne Terrace. There are Wayne State Universities in Michigan and Ohio; Anthony Wayne School Districts in both Ohio and Pennsylvania; several Anthony Wayne elementary schools; hundreds of highways, bridges and public structures; and Wayne National Forest.

There have been various books written about Wayne over the years, including some works of popular fiction. Only Theodore Roosevelt's *Winning of the West* has risen to classic status, and the movies have pretty much left Wayne alone, but we have plenty of Wayne reminders.

Hawkeye and the Battle of Fallen Timbers

In a series of novels written almost two hundred years ago, James Fenimore Cooper created the original American action hero, Natty Bumppo. Nathaniel Bumppo was also known as Hawkeye, La Longue Carabine, Deerslayer, Leatherstocking and several other names. He was the hero of five novels, the most famous being *The Last of the Mohicans*. There have been many film and television versions of this story, including the 1992 movie starring Daniel Day-Lewis. Many consider Hawkeye—skilled in combat with a variety of weapons, brave and resourceful—to be the first great American action hero. He also embodies the image of the lone frontiersman living on the edge of society and moving ever westward with his trusty long rifle.

Though the most popular of the five novels takes place during the French and Indian Wars, the final chapter of our hero's life is covered in *The Prairie*. *The Prairie* takes place in 1804, far west of the Mississippi. A party of pioneers find an eighty-year-old Natty Bumppo living in the wilderness, trapping and hanging out with the local Indians. Early in the book, the leader of the pioneers, a crusty old sort named Ismael Bush, brags about having served under Anthony Wayne. Natty replies, "I fou't my last battle, as I hope, under

64 THE PRAIRIE.

without the help of what is called the law. We ar' of a slow breed, it may be said, and it is often said of us; but slow is sure; and there ar' few men living who can say they ever struck a blow, that they did not get one as hard in return, from Ishmael Bush."

"Then has Ishmael Bush followed the instinct of the beasts, rather than the principle which ought to belong to his kind," returned the stubborn trapper. "I have struck many a blow myself, but never have I felt the same ease of mind that of right belongs to a man who follows his reason, after slaying even a fawn, when there was no call for his meat or hide, as I have felt at leaving a Mingo unburied in the woods, when following the trade of open and honest warfare."

"What, you have been a soldier, have you, trapper! I made a forage or two among the Cherokees, when I was a lad, myself; and I followed Mad Anthony,[1] one season, through the beeches; but there was altogether too much tattooing and regulating among his troops for me; so I left him, without calling on the paymaster to settle my arrearages. Though, as Esther afterwards boasted, she had made such use of the pay-ticket, that the States gained no great sum by the oversight. You have heard of such a man as Mad Anthony, if you tarried long among the soldiers."

"I fou't my last battle, as I hope, under his orders," returned the trapper, a gleam of sunshine shooting from his dim eyes, as if the event was recollected with pleasure, and then a sudden shade of sorrow succeeding, as though he felt a secret admonition against dwelling on the violent scenes in which he had so often been an actor. "I was passing from the States on the sea-shore into these far regions, when I crossed the trail of his army, and I fell in, on his rear, just as a looker-on; but when they got to blows, the crack of my rifle was heard among the rest, though to my shame it may be said, I never knew the right of the quarrel, as well as a man of threescore and ten should know the reason of his acts afore he takes mortal life, which is a gift he never can return!"

"Come, stranger," said the emigrant, his rugged nature

[1] Anthony Wayne, a Pennsylvanian distinguished in the war of the Revolution, and subsequently against the Indians of the West, for his daring as a general, by which he gained from his followers the title of Mad Anthony. General Wayne was the son of the person mentioned in the life of West, as commanding the regiment which excited his military ardor.

Left: Illustration for *Last of the Mohicans*, by N.C. Wyeth, 1909. *Public domain.*

Right: Hawkeye talks about Fallen Timbers. *Photo by author.*

his orders." He then relates how on his way west, he crossed Wayne's trail and followed it to Fallen Timbers, where "the crack of my rifle was heard among the rest." So there you have it: the greatest fictional frontiersman of all time fought his last battle right here.

John (Anthony) Wayne

A young actor appeared in 1930s Hollywood by the name of Marion Michael Morrison. He had a talent for Westerns, so the famous director Raoul Walsh thought that the young man needed a manly Western hero name. Walsh suggested he call himself Anthony Wayne. According to legend, a movie producer heard the name and objected to Anthony. He felt "Tony" was too Italian, so he changed Anthony to John. John Wayne rode off to star in 142 films, becoming one of America's favorite film frontiersmen.

Bruce Wayne

When DC Comics created the Batman series, they needed an old mansion and a backstory of wealth dating to the American Revolution. So the story goes that stately Wayne Manor was given by George Washington to one of his favorite generals as a reward for his service. Thus the house became the home of Anthony and, later, multimillionaire Bruce Wayne. Bruce Wayne is a direct descendant of Anthony Wayne. So the "mad" general lives on in modern pop culture as the Dark Knight.

Misplaced Monument or Monumental Vision

On a hill fifty feet above the Maumee River floodplain stands a massive statue of Anthony Wayne. On his left is a whiskered settler and, on his right, a Native American warrior. On the surface, the statue seems to tell a simple, traditional story of American history. Wayne stands taller than the other two and looks like a conqueror. The settler with his axe on his shoulder is ready to clear the land and tame the wilderness. The Indian holds a calumet or peace pipe and is ready to step out of the way. Seen another way, it tells a different story. The settler has his axe, but his left hand grips a rifle. Wayne's sword is high on his chest and clenched in his grip. The Native American may be holding a "peace pipe," but he still carries a musket.

The tension in the composition is enhanced by the men's stern facial expressions and the directions they are facing. The monument itself faces southeast. Wayne and the settler are looking to the left, due east, toward the place they came from and whence hordes of others are soon to come. The Indian is looking right, due South, toward lands he has lost.

The monument is the work of sculptor Bruce Saville. As a young man, Saville moved to Paris to study art. When the First World War broke out, Saville volunteered to serve in the French ambulance corps. When the United States entered the war, he transferred to the U.S. Army. His wartime experiences deeply influenced his work. In 1921, he moved to Columbus, Ohio, and became head of Ohio State's Department of Sculpture. Among the works he created at this time are *Peace*, which stands on the north lawn of the Ohio Statehouse, and *The Victorious Doughboy*, which stands in front of the Ohio History Connection Museum in Columbus. Both works dealt with the First World War and its aftermath.

The Fallen Timbers Battlefield Monument. *Photo by author.*

The Fallen Timbers Monument was commissioned by the Ohio Historical Society, now known as the Ohio History Connection, to celebrate the 135th anniversary of the battle. It was dedicated in 1929 on what was thought to be the battlefield. The society placed the monument on a nine-acre site along with a brass marker mounted on a stone listing the American killed and wounded. The dedication was a big deal. The floodplain below the monument was turned into a vast parking lot. The U.S. Postal service issued a two-cent commemorative stamp in honor of the event. There were speakers and hoopla.

After the Fallen Timbers Monument, Saville found a new passion. He moved to Santa Fe, New Mexico, to study Native American art and culture. In contrast to some of the stereotypical images on the base of the Fallen Timbers Monument, Saville produced beautiful and important works honoring Native Americans. He died in 1938 of influenza at the age of forty-six.

Meanwhile, back in Ohio, in the 1930s, the Works Progress Administration filled in the Miami-Erie canal and built US Route 24. The new monument on the new highway was a major tourist attraction. In 1953, Turkey Foot Rock was moved to the site. On the 200th anniversary of the battle, in 1994, a monument listing the tribes who fought in the battle was dedicated. In 1995, it was determined that the actual battle occurred north of Monument Park. There were immediate comments and editorials in the *Cleveland Plain*

A commemorative envelope with a Fallen Timbers stamp, mailed and postmarked the day of the dedication of the Fallen Timbers Battlefield Memorial. *Author's collection.*

Dealer and other news media about the monument being in the wrong place. Though it sparked some controversy, and one local businessman even suggested that the monument should be moved, popular opinion saw the monument on its nine-acre site as still very important to the story. In 1999, federal legislation was passed combining the Fallen Timber Battlefield Memorial Park, the Fallen Timbers Battlefield and the Fort Miamis site into one national park affiliate managed by the Toledo Metroparks.

In the master plan, the Toledo Metroparks refer to the Fallen Timbers Battlefield Memorial Park as a sacred, contemplative area, and it is. Yes, it is in the wrong spot, but that spot gives you a moving view of the Maumee River Valley, which vividly illustrates what everyone was really fighting over.

A Small Treat for History Fans

The first day of the 1995 archaeological survey of the Fallen Timbers Battlefield, Dr. Mike Pratt found a bayonet. It was of a type fitted for the Charleville musket carried by the U.S. Army. A search of the nearby area revealed no trace of the musket. In his lectures, Mike would speculate that the musket was dropped by a frightened or wounded soldier and found by an Indian. Native American warriors did not like bayonets, so the first thing he would have done was take the bayonet off and toss it aside.

The Fallen Timbers Monument Indian has a musket slung over his soldier. It has very distinct barrel bands, making it a Charleville. It's a captured American musket with no bayonet.

Anthony Wayne, the New Deal and Communication

In 1938, under President Roosevelt's New Deal, a new post office was built in Maumee on Conant Street and a mural commissioned. The oil on canvas mural was titled *Communication*. The artist, Rudolph Scheffler (1884–1973), specialized in creating murals, stained glass and mosaics for churches and synagogues. His created his most memorable art in the Ohio Supreme Court building, including all the murals in the courtroom, the mosaic panels depicting Ceres and Vulcan in the first-floor stairwells and the mosaic ceiling at the Front Street entrance.

Communication is an important piece of New Deal–era art, and when the new post office was built on Ford Street, the mural was removed, along with the

Left: Side view of the Fallen Timbers Monument showing the Native man carrying a captured musket. *Photo by author.*

Below: The WPA mural *Communication* in its current location in the conference room at the Maumee, Ohio post office. *Photo by author.*

1930s woodwork, and preserved. It currently hangs in the conference room of the Maumee Post Office on Ford Street, which is not open to the public.

Generations of Maumee residents have viewed the mural and wondered what it all means. Art interpretation is always a subjective area, but here is the interpretation I have put together. The Maumee mural features the goddess of communication, Iris. She communicated by air, symbolized by the eagle; by sea, symbolized by Poseidon's trident; and by land, symbolized by the horse. A god in a chariot is leaving, on the right, replaced by the new technology of the train and the telegraph, on the left. The eagle is similar to the National Recovery Administration's blue eagle symbol. In myths, Iris rides the rainbow, suggested here by the faint American flag. All this is made possible by Anthony Wayne forcing the Indian west. The Indian appears to be holding a treaty. In the mural's original location, the Indian was literally going west. The military might of the United States is symbolized by Wayne's fist. There is a lot to think about here. Love or hate it, it's history.

ENDURING LEGACIES

"The Honor of My Profession": The Battle That Didn't Happen

On April 8, 1794, a British ship sailed up the Maumee River and dropped anchor somewhere between modern-day Maumee and Perrysburg.[49] After studying the area for two days, Colonel John Graves Simcoe, governor of Upper Canada, chose the site for Fort Miamis. The location (in what is now Maumee, at the foot of Michigan Avenue) was on a slight rise above the river. Cannons in the fort controlled both the Maumee River and the great land trail north. Any attack on Detroit would have to go through Fort Miamis.

During the spring and summer of 1794, while Wayne was marching north, Simcoe scrambled to find troops and finish the fort. On the morning of August 20, the fort was still not completed. The garrison under the command of Major William Campbell consisted of approximately 160 English soldiers and fewer than 40 Canadian Rangers, and half of them were sick with malaria. In a dispatch sent to Detroit that evening, Campbell wrote: "We have passed a very odd kind of day." The soldiers at Fort Miamis heard the battle that morning. Later, they saw Indians moving past them heading toward Swan Creek (present-day downtown Toledo). Around eleven o'clock in the morning, Campbell ordered the garrison to stand to arms.

Native American Memorial at Fallen Timbers Battlefield. *Photo by author.*

The gates were barred, brush and obstacles were rolled into the ditches and the men were armed and at their combat posts. Then the Native Americans disappeared, and the situation got strangely quiet. General Wayne was authorized to take the fort "if necessary." Campbell was expected to defend his post "if attacked." Both commanders were authorized to fight, but only if the other guy started it.

The first day, the British could see the Americans moving in the woods and setting up camp upstream, but Wayne made no approach to the fort or any attempt to communicate with Campbell. On August 21, twenty-four hours after the battle, Campbell sent an officer out of the fort under a white flag with a letter for Wayne. This began an extraordinary exchange of letters in which each man, in the extremely polite style of the day, insulted and goaded the other. Campbell began by inquiring what an army "said to be under your command" was doing so close to his position. Wayne was incensed and waited until four o'clock in the afternoon to send a reply: "Were you entitled to an answer, the most full and satisfactory one was announced to you from the muzzles of my small arms, yesterday morning."

Wayne fumed while studying the fort and contemplated an attack. The fort was well built and mounted heavy guns. Wayne had won fame during the American Revolution for a daring night attack on a British strongpoint. Wayne, thinking of his past success, made a comment to his officers that maybe a night attack was called for. Inside the fort, Campbell was aware of Wayne's reputation and wrote, "I trust if he attacks us this night, he will not find us unprepared."[50]

On August 22, Wayne grew bolder. In the company of several officers, he rode up to the fort. Then he dismounted, walked up to within pistol range and inspected the earthworks. According to tradition, an angry English officer begged Campbell's permission to shoot him. Though deeply insulted, Campbell resorted to ink instead of gunpowder and wrote another angry letter. He promised Wayne that if he did that again, "my indispensable duty to my King and country, and honor of my profession, will oblige me to have recourse to those measures which thousands of either nation may hereafter have cause to regret." Wayne's response was to promise Campbell and his troops safe passage if they would lay down their arms and surrender.

The last letter from William Campbell, major, Twenty-Fourth Regiment, commanding at Fort Miamis, to Anthony Wayne, major general and commander-in-chief of the federal army, was polite and proper but said, in effect, "Hell no!"

On August 23, three days after the battle and after burning all the Indian crops, supplies and buildings on both sides of the river, Wayne drew up his army and held a ceremony for the men they had lost. The great federal army then withdrew.

Fort Miamis is remarkable not for the battle that was fought there but for the battle that was not fought there. Wayne's troops hated the English for giving guns and support to the Native Americans. At noon on August 20, they were fresh from the fight, fresh from being shot at or wounded, fresh from seeing their comrades killed. The illegal fort on American soil had to have outraged many. But there was no mad, bloody assault and no random sniping. They followed orders and held their fire. For the men inside the fort, the constant taunting by Americans riding in and out of musket range had to have been infuriating, even without Wayne's outrageous theatrics. It is amazing that when historians tell the story today they don't begin with, "We don't know who fired the first shot, but…" The story of Fort Miami in 1794 is a tribute to military discipline. Two angry armies stared at each other over loaded weapons for three days, and no one broke discipline, so everyone lived to fight another day. That is the miracle of Fort Miamis.

Some writers credit love of country or patriotism as the source of military discipline. When you look at someone like Major Campbell, who

Ruins of Fort Miamis. Postcard circa 1910. *Author's collection.*

was a Scot commanding a regiment of Welsh soldiers in the service of an English king in North America, discipline may have been less about national identity and more about what Major Campbell called "the honor of my profession."

A copy of Wayne and Campbell's letters can be found at the Internet Archive.[51]

Campbell and Wayne: The Last Campaign

If I die in a combat zone
Box me up and ship me home
Pin my medals across my chest
And tell my mother I did my best.
—U.S. Army marching cadence

Military expeditions into foreign lands take a heavy toll. Unknown dangers, strange illnesses and a change of climate can be as deadly as the enemy. The Fallen Timbers campaign was no exception. I previously talked about the dramatic exchange between Major General Anthony Wayne, commander of the Army of the United States, and Major William Campbell, commander of British forces, at Fort Miamis. In a little-known twist of fate, Fallen

Timbers was destined to be the last campaign for both Wayne and Campbell and may have killed them both. While the Native leaders, fighting on their home ground, lived for many years after the battle, Wayne and Campbell had very little time left.

Major William Campbell was a Scot descended from the Duke of Argyll.[52] He was a professional soldier in the British army who saw action during the American War for Independence. In 1794, he was in command of a company of the Twenty-Fourth Regiment of Foot at Detroit. His small force was supplemented by about ten members of the royal artillery, a handful of soldiers from the Fifth Regiment of Foot, a few Royal Marines, some Canadian militia forces and a group of French militia from the Frenchtown (Monroe, Michigan) area. With this makeshift army, Campbell was ordered into the Ohio Territory.

Construction on Fort Miamis began in the spring of 1794. By summer, many of the men were stricken with an illness attributed to the foul air and water of the place. It was probably malaria. Campbell, at the age of forty-three, was also taken seriously ill with a fever.

Wayne started the Fallen Timbers campaign with health problems. At forty nine years of age, he was overweight, liked to drink and suffered from gout. The afternoon of August 2, 1794, found Wayne in camp on the Saint Mary River in western Ohio. He had retired to his tent for an afternoon nap when a tree came crashing down on him. Though Wayne was stunned and shaken, the only injury he suffered was a blow to his left leg. The injury from the falling tree made his gout worse. By August 20, the day of the battle, he was walking with difficulty and had to be lifted into his saddle. Nonetheless, his forces defeated the Indian confederacy and moved to within striking distance of Fort Miamis.

The following day, Wayne, nursing an injured leg, and Campbell, weakened from the fever, confronted each other and exchanged a series of angry letters, almost starting a war. Ironically, this exchange would make both men heroes. Wayne was seen as standing up to the British Empire and tweaking the nose of the English lion. Campbell was honored for his bravery and professionalism in holding his own at the frontier outpost despite being cut off from support and vastly outnumbered. Campbell was promoted to lieutenant colonel, and in 1795, he returned briefly to England and received a "public expression of thanks from the traders of London, whose interest were much concerned in the conflict."[53] The same year, Wayne negotiated the Treaty of Greenville, which opened the Northwest Territory to settlement by the United States.

In 1796, Campbell received another promotion and was sent to Bermuda as governor. Meanwhile, back in the Northwest Territory, Wayne took possession of Campbell's former post, Fort Miamis, and on August 13, he arrived in Detroit. After a triumphant occupation of the former British city, Wayne decided to head home. On November 17, he boarded a ship and sailed east.

On Lake Erie, Wayne's left leg, injured in 1794, began to swell and cause him terrible pain. He was forced to stop at Fort Presque Isle (current-day Erie, Pennsylvania). At the same time, Colonel Campbell arrived in Bermuda. Within a few days, his fever returned, and he fell ill. By December, both men were bedridden. As the two professional soldiers lay dying in remote frontier outposts, it is unlikely that either man knew anything of the other's fate.

Campbell died on December 2. Wayne followed thirteen days later, on December 15. The rigors of the Fallen Timbers campaign almost certainly shortened the life of both men.

Campbell was buried in St. Peter's Church, St. George's, Bermuda. The church, founded in 1612, is the oldest continuously used Protestant church in the western hemisphere. Campbell's grieving widow paid one of the best sculptors in England to carve a memorial. Thousands of tourists pass though the church every year, and probably a few pause to read the memorial on

St. Peter's Church, Bermuda. UNESCO World Heritage Site. *Shutterstock. by Yingna Cai.*

Left: Campbell Memorial. Sculptor, John Bacon. *Courtesy of JoeyBagODonuts via Wikimedia Commons.*

Opposite, top: William Eaton. *From* Naval Documents related to United States War with the Barbary Powers September 7, 1804 through April 1805 *(United States Government Printing Office).*

the wall and wonder, "Who was William Campbell, governor and lieutenant colonel of the Twenty-Fourth Regiment of Foot?"

Historians have noted that conquest comes with a high price, and it is often paid by men such as Wayne and Campbell.

Fallen Timbers and the United States Marine Corps

There were no marines at the Battle of Fallen Timbers, but there are connections between Anthony Wayne and the marines.

William Eaton (February 23, 1764–June 1, 1811), served as a captain in Wayne's army. A supporter of Wayne, he was one of his best recruiters. Eaton was a vital part of the training and formation of Wayne's Legion. After beginning a career in the Wayne's army, he went into politics and diplomacy. Eaton was a colorful and controversial character. He served as consul general to Tunis under Thomas Jefferson.

Eaton became a player in the war against the Barbary pirates. The U.S. Navy had blockaded the port of Tripoli and was content to wait it out. Eaton urged an invasion by land. The navy said no. Eventually, Eaton convinced the navy (or they got tired of arguing with him), and they agreed to let him go ashore and try to raise an army among enemies of the Barbary pirates.

The navy gave Eaton an escort of eight Marines. On April 27, 1805, Eaton's forces attacked and took control of the city of Derne. In the words of historian Spencer Tucker, "Captain Presley O'Bannon of the U.S. Marine Corps raised the American flag for the first time over a conquered foreign city." At the Battle of Derne, one marine was killed, and two were wounded. Eaton was wounded in the left wrist. The pirates sued for peace. A Wayne veteran was present on the shores of Tripoli.

The Uniform That Wouldn't Die

In 1792, Anthony Wayne created the U.S. Army, as well as a unique uniform for it. In 1796, Wayne died, and James Wilkinson, the new commander, did away with the legion system and redesigned the uniforms. A few years later, when Jefferson rebuilt the navy, the newly revived marines needed uniforms. Unused Wayne uniforms were found in storage and issued to the marines. The marines added a black leather piece that went around the neck and were nicknamed leathernecks, a term the marines use to this day. Over two hundred years and many modifications later, the U.S. Marine Corps dress blue uniform is the most honored and recognized uniform in history. It is also the only U.S. uniform to still incorporate the red, white and blue.

USMC dress blues. *By Captain Donna Neary, USMCR, for mil/news/publications/public domain.*

Wayne's Legion reenactors. *Photo by author.*

Fallen Timbers, Birthplace of the U.S. Military

In times of war and not before,
God and the soldier we adore.
But in times of peace and all things righted,
God is forgotten and the soldier slighted.
—Rudyard Kipling

Supporting the military is as American as apple pie. That was not always the case. Many of our founding fathers felt that the United States would be just fine without an army or a navy. The army that fought the revolution was a temporary combination of state units and militia loosely organized as the Continental Army. When the war ended in 1783, the Continental Congress lost no time in disbanding the army and selling off the few ships that made up the navy. On June 2, 1784, all but eighty men, a clerk and a few officers were discharged. Warehouses full of weapons and supplies were locked and left unguarded. The navy and the marines were sent home.[54]

The reason for trashing an army that had served so well were fear, greed and power. Though few Americans today know anything about Oliver Cromwell, his presence haunted eighteenth-century Englishmen and the former Englishmen who were our founding fathers. Cromwell was a seventeenth-century military leader who developed an efficient, modernized army. In 1649, he used it to overthrow King Charles the First and, in 1653, make himself dictator of England. England experienced sixty years of instability and bloodshed as a result. While fear that a strong military can result in a military dictatorship is a legitimate concern, there were more selfish concerns motivating many of the men debating the future of the new nation. Armies and navies are extremely expensive. They require taxes, and many of the founders were just plain cheap. They found the idea of any taxes repugnant. There was also the question of power. Many state officials feared creating a strong federal government with the ability to tax them. Some had legitimate philosophical opposition to a strong government, but many acted out of narrow-minded self-interest.

Without military backup, Americans found themselves at the mercy of pirates at sea, Indians on the frontier and outlaws almost everywhere. By the time of the Constitutional Convention in 1787, there was agreement among the founders that the new country needed a new military. The argument then became about what kind of military. Two schools of thought emerged. Washington, Hamilton and the Federalists believed

DEFEAT of the INDIANS.

In the laſt CENTINEL an account of the defeat of the Indians by the Kentucky volunteers was announced, as received from *Philadelphia*.—The accounts from the frontiers are ſo various and contradictory, that it is with caution, we publiſh them. Of this report we have, however, received the following corroborative particulars.

Hagarſtown, Sept. "I congratulate yon on the news of the defeat of the Indians by the *Kentucky* volunteers."

Frederick, Sept. 16. "Advices f om the weſtward, received by a gentleman of veracity, who arrived in this town on Monday laſt, announce, that General SCOTT, having under his command upwards of 1400 men, four miles in advance of General WAYNE's army, was ſuddenly attacked by a conſiderable number of Indians: that after a ſevere conflict of 45 minutes, the Indians were totally routed leaving behind them upwards of 200 dead on the ſpot. We are ſorry to add, that the loſs ſuſtained by General SCOTT, amounts, in killed, wounded and miſſing, to 384, among them ſome brave, enterprizing officers."

Gov. LEE, of *Virginia*, is appointed to the Chief command of the troops gone againſt the inſurgents in the back parts of *Pennſylvania*.

Left: A newspaper account of the Battle of Fallen Timbers, fictionalized for political reasons. In this version (published in Boston), the Kentucky militia charged ahead and defeated the Indians while Wayne and the regulars did nothing, four miles in the rear. *Author's collection.*

Below: *Columbian Centinel*, October 1, 1794. *Author's collection.*

Columbian  Centinel.

Printed and publiſhed on *WEDNESDAYS* and *SATURDAYS*, by BENJAMIN RUSSELL, in STATE-STREET, *Boſton*, (*Maſſachuſetts.*)

Whole No. 1099.] *WEDNESDAY*, OCTOBER 1, 1794. [No. 7, *of* VOL. XXII.

Sales at Auction.

Will be ſold at Public Auction,

This Day,

At 11 o'clock on the Premiſes,

THE Real Eſtate of DAVID BELL, ſen. deceaſed, conſiſting of a convenient DWELLING-HOUSE, ſituated in Croſs-Street, bounding on the Mill-Pond, with a ſmall TENEMENT adjoining, having a good well of water in the yard. The particulars of payment and poſſeſſion will be made known at the time of ſale.

JONAS WELSH, *Adminiſtrator.*

TAKE NOTICE.

Will be ſold by Public Auction,

On Wedneſday, 15th October next,

THE following REAL ESTATE, in the town of Cambridge, late the property of Dr. EDWARD WIGGLESWORTH, deceaſed, viz.

1. A Dwelling-Houſe and Out-Houſes, with about 5 acres of Land adjoining, pleaſantly ſituated near the Meeting-Houſe, on the road to Weſt-Boſton Bridge. The front on ſaid road is 190 feet, and the preſent Dwelling-Houſe is ſo ſituated as conveniently to admit another.

2. A Lot of Land, containing 6 acres, and nearly 3 quarters of an acre, ſituated on the road to Watertown, oppoſite the dwelling-houſe of JOSEPH LEE, Eſq. having a front on ſaid road of about 60 rods.

3. A Lot of Land, containing 5 acres, adjoining land of the Hon. Judge DANA, a few rods North-Eaſt of his Dwelling-Houſe.

4. A Lot of Land, containing about 8 acres, ſituated at a ſmall diſtance Northward the lot juſt mentioned.

5. A Lot of Land, containing about 8 acres, ſituated on Cambridge-Neck, ſo called, nearly oppoſite the dwelling-houſe of LEONARD JARVIS, Eſq. being one lot back from the road to Weſt-Boſton Bridge.

6. A Meadow-Lot, in Freſh Pond meadows, containing one acre and an half, adjoining lots of Major JNO. PALMER.

7. One other Lot in ſaid Meadows, containing about two acres.

Miſcellany.

FOR THE COLUMBIAN CENTINEL.

MR. RUSSELL,

The following addreſs of Mr. SMITH, contains a ſummary view of the reaſons and motives by which the Federal party in Congreſs were influenced, during the laſt Seſſion. It has appeared in the Southern papers; but I do not remember to have ſeen it in any of ours this way. The ſubject is certainly very intereſting to your readers, and is treated with great ability by the writer—and I am perſuaded you would ſerve the cauſe of your country, and gratify many of your cuſtomers by the republication of this addreſs in the CENTINEL. It will be remembered that it was written for the peruſal of his immediate conſtituents.

HORTENSIUS.

An ADDRESS from

William Smith, of South-Carolina,

To his CONSTITUENTS.

TO promote the welfare and proſperity of his country is the firſt duty of every citizen who is inveſted with a public truſt; to conciliate the eſteem of his fellow citizens in general, and thoſe in particular by whom he is entruſted, is the next.—Fortunate is he who by his conduct can unite two objects ſo intereſting and ſo deſirable: But it too frequently happens that they are irreconcileable to each other, and that in the conflict of ſentiments ariſing from political circumſtances, the public man muſt make his election either to ſacrifice his conſcience to his popularity, or his popularity to his conſcience.

Theſe ideas are intended as an introduction to an addreſs to my conſtituents, which ſome recent information, relative to their opinions, has ſuggeſted as neceſſary in the exiſting criſis of our public affairs. In free governments, the repreſentative is bound to explain to the repreſented, whenever they require it, the grounds and motives of his conduct. It is eſſential to their ſatisfaction that they ſhould,

Were it true that I had advocated the cauſe of the Britiſh nation and vindicated her piratical conduct, no reproach could have been too harſh for ſuch treachery. But let us ſtate the thing truly, and then the ſyllogiſm would ſtand thus:—"Commercial reſtrictions were propoſed, which were thought by many of the moſt reſpectable characters in the United States to be pregnant with miſchievous conſequences to the commercial & agricultural intereſt of this country; it was the duty of thoſe who viewed them in that light to oppoſe them—he did oppoſe them—therefore he has done what his duty dictated."

Thus ſtands the ſyllogiſm as to the *fact*; how ſhould it ſtand as to the *arguments and principles* by which the oppoſition was conducted: Thus—a ſyſtem of commercial regulations was propoſed favourable to *France*, injurious to *Britain*, predicated upon a ſyſtem of commerce on the part of *France* favourable to the United States, and on the part of *Britain*, unfavourable to the United States—the reverſe being the truth, it was the duty of thoſe who knew the reverſe to be true to ſhew it;—he proved it by an undeniable ſtatement of facts; he did therefore nothing more than duty preſcribed. Connecting the two foregoing ſtatements they form this reſult; that the ſubject was merely a *commercial* one, and the inquiry, 1ſt. Whether the French or the Britiſh commercial ſyſtem was on the whole moſt beneficial to the United States; 2d. Whether the propoſed regulations in a commercial point of view were likely to prove injurious or not?

It was my opinion, that the *commercial ſyſtem* of *Great-Britain*, was, on the whole, more favourable to the United States than the *permanent commercial ſyſtem of France*; it likewiſe appeared to me, from the beſt documents, that the deviations from the latter, were in general, either dictated by the neceſſity of the moment, or leſs favourable to us than the original ſyſtem. 2d. It was my opinion, that the propoſed reſtrictions

er came to be developed and underſtood, the advocates for the propoſitions, finding that the *commercial* ground was untenable, and that the *facts* which had been ſtated and the inferrences ariſing from them had made an impreſſion which threatened the rejection of their favourite project, reſorted to their *political* ground.

This corps de reſerve being now brought into play, a furious charge was made upon the paſſions and feelings of the Houſe with the Indians, the Algerines, the weſtern poſts, the violations of our neutral rights, the ſpoliations on our commerce.

Having preſcribed to myſelf from the beginning, a line which I firmly reſolved not to tranſgreſs, I made no reply whatever to theſe arguments, I conſidered them as inapplicable to the ſubject, that we were diſcuſſing a *peace* ſyſtem, and that if *war* were to be reſorted to, other meaſures of a very different complexion would be expedient. In my reply, therefore, I confined myſelf as I had done before, to the *commercial part of the arguments*; I did not meddle with the political topics introduced, nor did I advance any thing which could by the tongue of calumny itſelf be miſconſtrued into a vindication of any of thoſe political injuries of *Great-Britain* which either exiſted before or which have grown out of the preſent war.

Other members however, did not ſuffer thoſe points to paſs unnoticed. They obſerved, that if it were true that *Great-Britain* had inflicted all theſe injuries on the *United States*, and ſhould refuſe to enter into ſuch amicable arrangements as would remove the grievances and afford ample redreſs, then it would be proper at once either to interdict all commercial intercourſe with that country or declare war againſt her; that with reſpect to the *Indians*, whatever ſuſpicions might be entertained, yet Congreſs had not ſufficient evidence that the Indian war was fomented by *Britain*, and if they had, the uſage of nations required that a complaint ſhould be made, before acts of hoſtility were recur-

a strong United States military under federal control was the only way to go. Staunch anti-Federalists such as Massachusetts Representative Elbridge Gerry and many southerners believed a system of well-regulated state militias could do the job. The local militia concept was especially popular among slave owners. An unspoken part of our early history is the prevailing fear of a slave revolt in the South. It was not an unfounded fear. Historian Herbert Aptheke, in his pioneering study *American Negro Slave Revolts* (1943), "found records of approximately two hundred and fifty revolts and conspiracies in the history of American Negro slavery." It was believed that a well-trained, well-armed local militia could respond more quickly to a slave insurrection than a federal army. It was also argued that local frontier militias could mobilize quickly and act decisively against Indian raids. The theory was sound, but it did not work in practice.

Funding, training and maintaining local militias turned out to be almost impossible. Local authorities did not have the money. As a result, militias were consistently underfunded, underequipped, undermanned and undertrained. During Harmar's 1790 campaign, militiamen panicked at the first shots and ran into the line of regulars, causing confusion, death and defeat. During the Battle of the Wabash, the Native forces intentionally attacked the militia camp first, literally stampeding them through the regulars' camp.

When Washington found the money and authorized Anthony Wayne to build and train a regular army, he was taking a big risk. If Wayne failed, the anti-federal forces were poised to cut funding, dismantle the army and go back to a temporary militia-based military. Wayne had no intention of failing. His men were extensively drilled and trained. While he used mounted militia to secure his flanks, the center of Wayne's line was the regulars. He also authorized his field officers to fire on the militia if they panicked, ran or in any way interfered with the army. The performance of Wayne's regulars at the Battle of Fallen Timbers was outstanding. Though the arguments continued, and the militia concept was tried again and again, the U.S. Army remained a strong and powerful force. It is no exaggeration to say that the mighty U.S. military was born on August 20, 1794. While Wayne was still in the Maumee Valley, construction started on six new U.S. warships. Three years after the Battle of Fallen Timbers, U.S. sailors and marines would once more take to the sea. The greatest of these ships was named to represent the power Wayne had fought for. It was, and is, the USS *Constitution.*

Without Due Honors: The Men Wayne Left Behind

On August 20, 1794, Wayne drove his men through the smoke of battle to pursue the fleeing Native Americans. His dead and dying were left where they fell. When the Americans made camp for the night, two officers and few others were buried in unmarked graves in what is now downtown Maumee, Ohio. The next day, a few wounded men were found or managed to wander into the American camp. It was not until August 22 that Wayne sent a small detachment back to the battlefield to bury the dead. Only nineteen bodies were found in the thick brush. They were quickly covered with rocks and brush or buried in shallow graves. Two wounded soldiers, Sergeant Eli Edmondson of the Fourth Legion Light Infantry and an unnamed private, are believed to have survived for two days on the battlefield, exposed to the animals and August heat. Sergeant Edmondson died just before being found, and the private died moments after being brought into camp. Wayne's jealous subordinate, James Wilkinson, looking for a way to discredit Wayne, jumped on this disregard for the dead and wounded. Wilkinson wrote that men were "left to ferment upon the surface, the prey of vultures, until the 22nd….For a single Man sacrificed by such cruel negligence, a General deserves to hanged, damned he certainly will be."[55]

Wayne's attitude toward his dead and wounded was typical of the military practices of the era. Care of the wounded and burying and identifying the dead were low priorities in an eighteenth-century army. Ceremony and honors were generally reserved for officers. A humble infantryman would have been lucky to get a marked grave. Dead soldiers were often piled in mass graves or, in contested areas, left to rot.

In July 1755, a British army under the command of General Edward Braddock was defeated by a French and Indian force near modern-day Pittsburgh. For twenty-six years, travelers complained about the bones on the road to Pittsburgh. It was not until 1781 that local farmers gathered them up and dumped them in a common grave. An even sadder spot was Fort Ticonderoga in upper New York State. More than two thousand British soldiers and American militia died there in a 1758 attack on the French garrison. Nearly twenty years later, during the American Revolution, the remote outpost was manned by a small group of Americans under the command of young Colonel Anthony Wayne. Wayne called the place "an ancient Golgotha or place of skulls—they are so plenty here that our people for want of other vessels drink out of them whilst the soldiers make tent pins out of the shins and thigh bones."[56]

Given that background, it is probably not surprising that Wayne had a hard attitude toward his own dead. Wilkinson's complaints about Wayne and the soldiers left on the field were widely circulated by writers in the eastern press. It was the only stain on a remarkable campaign. Wilkinson's smear campaign did not accomplish his goals, but the discussion may have prompted a rethinking of old attitudes. Beginning in the early 1800s, army quartermasters were charged with the job of properly identifying and burying soldiers who died at frontier outposts. It was a small start, but it was a start nonetheless.

During the American Civil War, the public began to put real pressure on the military to identify the dead and bury them properly. Still, only 58 percent of the Civil War dead were ever identified. For the families of the missing, this was intolerable. That led to changes. In 1988, Dr. Steven E. Anders, quartermaster corps historian, wrote,

> *Beginning with a change of sensibilities, with the consciousness that soldiers and their families did not want the fate or the identity of those who fell in battle to be unknown, there has been a continual effort to improve the techniques, equipment, doctrine and organizations designated to care for the Army's dead.*[57]

A member of the Old Guard, Third U.S. Infantry, standing guard at the Tomb of the Unknown Soldier. *CC0, public domain.*

Today, soldiers in the Quartermasters Mortuary Affairs Service are active around the world identifying and bringing home the remains of Americans killed in action in past and present conflicts. According to the army, 96 percent of the fallen from the Vietnam War have been identified. With modern technology and commitment from the military to leave no one behind, it may yet be possible to identify and pay honor to every soldier, sailor, marine or airman who falls. There will be no more unknowns.

Nowhere is the importance of honoring our war dead more important than at the Tomb of the Unknowns in Arlington National Cemetery. The tomb is guarded twenty-four hours a day by members of the Third U.S. Infantry Regiment, known as the Old Guard.

They also do ceremonial duties and burials at Arlington. There is a small guard shelter at the tomb. During one hundred years of guarding the tomb, there have been several occasions, during blizzards and hurricanes, when the sentinel was given the option of standing guard in the shelter and not walking the post. According to Old Guard tradition, that has never happened. The post has been walked continually for one hundred years.

More than two centuries ago, an unknown wounded soldier suffered for two days before being found. He then died and was buried in an unmarked grave in what is now Maumee, Ohio. For a moment, his story was national news. It is impossible to say if his ordeal had any impact on attitudes toward the fallen, but it is worth noting that he was a member of the First U.S. Legion, a unit that still exists today as the Third U.S., the Old Guard.

Blood Ties: Shannon and the Chief

Dr. Shannon Hughes. *Photo by Amber Breault-Albain.*

If you grew up watching Western movies and TV shows in the twentieth century, you were lied to. Many, if not most, of the Indians you saw on the screen were not Native Americans. It's more likely they were Italians. Hollywood had a preference for casting Italians as Indians. In a July 23, 2006 article in the *Los Angeles Times*, Howard Mann quotes a casting director as saying, "We only use Italians for Indian parts. They look more Indian than the Indians." This next story, though, is different; it is about an Italian American girl who found out she was really a Native American woman.

Our story starts over two hundred years ago, where the St. Joseph and the St. Marys River join to form the Maumee River. The Miami village there was called Kekionga. The Miami at Kekionga controlled an eight-mile portage between the Maumee and the Wabash River. This small portage connected the Great Lakes to the Mississippi River. This link was crucial to French, English and Native American trade routes. The chief of the village was a Miami named Pacanne (P'Koum-Kwa).[58] Pacanne was the principle chief and probably the most influential leader of the Miami people. He was described as a businessman who saw to the welfare of his people. He traveled extensively throughout the Ohio, Indiana and Illinois areas. When he was

Pacanne, chief of the Miami, by Henry Hamilton. *Houghton Library, Harvard College.*

absent, he often left his sister Tacumwah in charge—a fact that was often remarked upon by whites.

Pacanne and Tacumwah had inherited the rights to the very lucrative portage. Tacumwah married a Frenchman and had four children with him. Her husband, Antoine Richardville, and two associates attempted to take control of the portage. The argument turned heated, and Richardville beat Tacumwah. She was sheltered by another French trader, named Charles Beaubien. Pacanne threatened to kill his brother-in-law but was restrained. The Frenchman still claimed rights, through his marriage, to the portage. In an unusual move, Pacanne and Tacumwah went to the English court in Detroit. On September 18, 1774, the court upheld that Tacumwah had inherited the business and property from her mother and declared that her husband had no claim on anything she owned. In an era when white women seldom had property rights, a court upholding the property rights of a Native woman against a European man was stunning. Tacumwah also got a divorce.

Despite his reputation as a businessman and a negotiator, Pacanne was also a feared warrior. In 1778, he accompanied British Governor Henry Hamilton on an expedition up the Maumee and down the Wabash to Vincennes, Indiana. There were some Piankeshaw chiefs who were sympathetic to the Americans. Pacanne sent them a message telling them Hamilton was coming and advising them to listen to this man. When they again spoke in favor of the Americans, Pacanne told them, "You should listen to this man." The interpreters told Hamilton that the first time, it was a suggestion; the second time, it was a threat.

In 1780, a Frenchman named La Balme, acting on behalf of the Americans, attacked Kekionga. Pacanne was away with a hunting party at the time. He returned, and while Miami War Chief Little Turtle attacked the main body of La Balme's army on the Eel River, Pacanne and his men quickly killed the party left to hold Kekionga. Pacanne then addressed the French who lived with and did business with the Miami: "You see our village stained with blood, you can think that we are not going to extend the hand to your friends who are our enemies. You can understand that if we find you with them that we will not make any distinction."

Pacanne fought in every battle of the Indian wars, including the Battle of Fallen Timbers. Always the protector and the organizer, he was never the star. He was overshadowed by the tactical brilliance of Little Turtle and strong personality of a fellow Miami chief named Nagohquangogh, or Le Gris. Pacanne felt betrayed by the Americans and refused to sign the Greenville Treaty, though he encouraged others to do so. He did not encourage the young Tecumseh in his resistance to the white man. Pacanne moved into central Indiana on the Mississinewa River. He attempted to remain neutral during the War of 1812, but when the Americans began attacking his villages, he went to war one more time. He died in 1816. He had a daughter who married a Frenchman.

Almost two centuries later, Shannon Hughes, fresh out of college, got a job at the Toledo Area Metroparks. Her dark hair and dark eyes were attributed to her father's Italian heritage. As the Metroparks grew, so did her job responsibilities. Shannon was drawn to the new, undeveloped Fallen Timbers Battlefield. She became the Metropark liaison for Fallen Timbers and was put in charge of relations with the Native American tribes. Almost two hundred years after the death of Pacanne, the Fallen Timbers Battlefield was opened to the public. Due in part to Shannon, Native Americans have been involved in every aspect of the development and interpretation of the battlefield.

While Shannon's responsibilities with the Metroparks continued to grow, she found time to earn a doctorate. Her job as director of education and programming encompasses the entire park system, but she continues to personally oversee the Fallen Timbers Battlefield. In 2020, during the COVID-19 lockdown and while recovering from a serious illness, she began researching her genealogy. The first thing she discovered is that she has very old French Canadian roots on her mother's side. Then she learned something incredible: her several times great-grandmother was the daughter of Pacanne. The woman who has defended the battlefield all these years is a descendant of a man who fought there. A lot of people might consider this a remarkable coincidence; Pacanne would probably say that it was fate.

EPILOGUE

Long ago, I read a novel called *Lost Man's River*, by the late Peter Mattissen. It is set in the Florida Everglades. The plot involves a man researching events that happened almost one hundred years earlier. While interviewing a very old Native man, a Miccosukee, he is told that one of his own ancestors was involved. "What a coincidence!" the young man exclaims. The old Miccosukee laughs at him: "Coincidence is a white man's word; there is no such thing."

The Lost Battlefield

On August 23, 1794, three days after the battle, Wayne's army moved back upriver. He paused at the battle site and had his men do a quick sweep to look for dropped equipment and, presumably, to throw a few rocks and dirt over any American bodies they found. A little later, British Indian agent Alexander McKee viewed the site. He was livid over the way the Americans had mutilated the bodies of the fallen Native Americans. Then, except for sad groups of Indians looking for their dead, the battlefield fell silent. There were no ruined buildings, no wrecked wagons or large debris—just trees, bones and spent bullets. The fallen trees rotted, new ones grew and nature took over. The place where hundreds of men fought and many still lay was lost to the spirits.

By the time white settlers started moving into the area, there was no sign that a battle had ever happened. But history, like nature, abhors a vacuum. The stories began. Storytellers took the poetic phrase "by the banks of the Maumee" literally. A rock along the river, with turkey foot petroglyphs, became a central part of the legends. By the 1920s, the story was that the battle was fought on the floodplain along the Maumee River. The Ohio Historical Society (now Ohio History Connection) built a monument in 1929 overlooking the floodplain. And for two hundred years, the real battlefield was forgotten.

In the 1980s, an archaeologist named Micheal Pratt was doing a dig at the site of Fort Miamis. As he worked, his mind kept returning to the story of the battle and its inconsistencies. He knew there was not enough room on that floodplain for two armies to maneuver. It also did not make sense to fight there, below a bluff, when you could command everything from the top of the bluff. Mike was bothered and couldn't let it go. A person raised in an Indigenous culture might have seen Mike's obsession as a message from the old ones, saying, "Let us find the truth."

Mike did get permission to survey the floodplain. He found nineteenth- and twentieth-century junk and plenty of pre-contact Native artifacts but nothing from the battle. He even found the burial site of an ancient man. The old one was buried with precious items indicating that in his time, he was a holy man or a shaman.[59] Obviously, the archaeologist was being told to look elsewhere.

Mike Pratt dove into battle research and developed a theory that the battle happened on land owned by the City of Toledo inside the City of Maumee. Despite intense political issues, permission for an archaeological study was granted; in the summer of 1995, it began. To my knowledge, Mike Pratt is not a superstitious man or given to flights of fancy, but after the first day of the study, even he had to wonder about divine intervention. That day, a bayonet unique to Anthony Wayne's infantry was found on the surface, and the earth began to give up artifact after artifact. By the end of the summer, there was no doubt the lost battlefield had been found.

In 1999, the battlefield, along with the monument site and the ruins of Fort Miamis, became an affiliated National Park managed by the Toledo Area Metroparks. In 2015, after twenty years of struggle, the battlefield was opened to the public. Descendants of the men who fought there, white and Native American, now visit the site. As a volunteer with the Metroparks, I have had the honor of meeting some of these individuals and hearing their stories. I have also heard many other stories of visions, spirits and unlikely "coincidences." Some are silly and easily explained. Some are not.

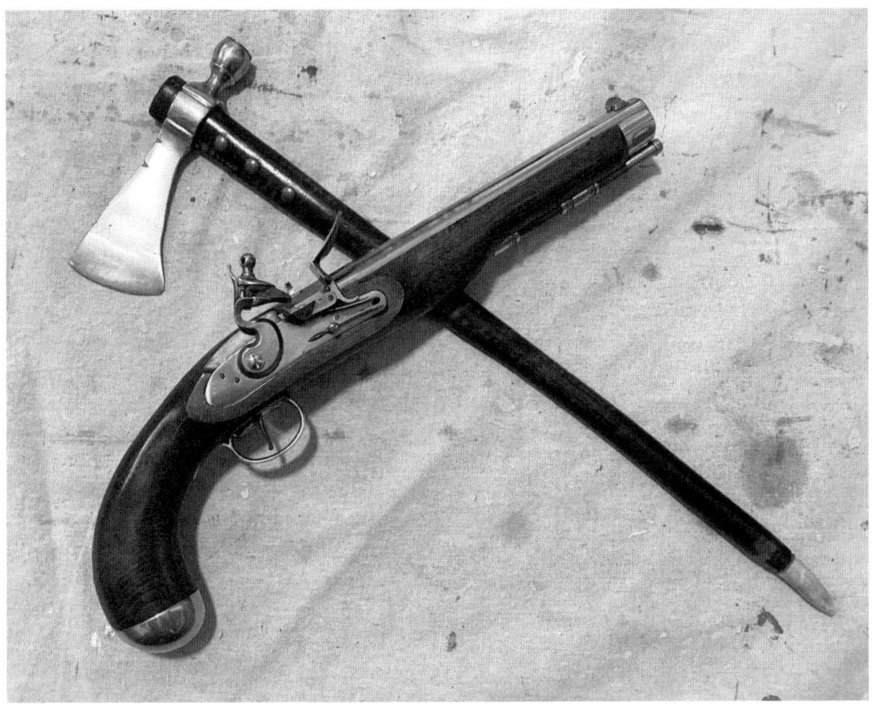

Photo by author.

I am not an especially religious man, but I know that when I walk the battlefield, the spirits of the past are present. I like to think they are now content. The place where they died is recognized, their struggles are remembered and their story is finally being told.

NOTES

Chapter 1

1. John Sugden, *Blue Jacket: Warrior of the Shawnees* (University of Nebraska Press, 2000), 169.
2. C.A. Buser, *Tarhe: Grand Sachem* (privately printed, 1978). Available via the Internet Archive.
3. Lenape Chief Buckongahelas, "Address to Christian Native Americans at Gnadenhutten," delivered in 1781, Gnadenhutten, Ohio. Available at American Rhetoric, https://www.americanrhetoric.com.
4. Wiley Sword, *President Washington's Indian War* (University of Oklahoma Press, 1985), 330.
5. Dresden Howard Papers, Fulton County Historical Society.
6. Colin G. Calloway, *The Indian World of George Washington* (Oxford University Press, 2018), 459.
7. C. Fayne Porter, *Battle of a Thousand Slain* (Scholastic Book Services, 1964), 60.

Chapter 2

8. Sword, *President Washington's Indian War*, 108.
9. Indiana Historical Bureau, "Site of Hardin's Defeat," https://www.in.gov.
10. Find a Grave, "Maj Alexander Trueman," https://www.findagrave.com.
11. "Pension Application of Alexander Truman (Trueman)," https://revwarapps.org/blwt2156-300.pdf.
12. See American State Papers, *Indian Affairs*, vol. 1, page 243, at https://www.govinfo.gov/content/pkg/SERIALSET-00524_00_00-122-0121-0000/pdf/SERIALSET-00524_00_00-122-0121-0000.pdf.
13. Steven P. Locke, *War Along the Wabash* (Casemate, 2023), 241.
14. Alan D. Gaff, *Bayonets in the Wilderness* (University of Oklahoma Press, 2004), 187.
15. Find a Grave, "Maj Alexander Trueman."
16. Gaff, *Bayonets in the Wilderness*, 9.

17. Susan Sleeper Smith, *Indigenous Prosperity and American Conquest: Indian Women of the Ohio River Valley, 1690–1792* (*Omohundro Institute of Early American History and Culture and the* University of North Carolina Press, 2018), 267.
18. Gaff, *Bayonets in the Wilderness*, 314.
19. Tricia A. Barbagallo, *Politicians Spill Blood on Albany Street*: New York Archives, Vol. 7 no. 1, Summer 2007 available at http://webarchive.loc.gov/all/20090519202131/http://www.archives.nysed.gov/apt/magazine/archivesmag_sum07.pdf
20. Sword, *President Washington's Indian War*, 211.

Chapter 3

21. Juliette Kinzie, *Wau-Bun: The Early Day in the Northwest* (Arcadia Publishing, 2010).
22. Gaff, *Bayonets in the Wilderness*, 8.
23. Linai T. Helm, *The Fort Dearborn Massacre* (Rand McNally, 1912). Available via Project Gutenberg.

Chapter 4

24. Frederick Wulff, *Alexander McKee: The Great White Elk* (Outskirts Press, 2013), 355.
25. Larry Nelson, *A Man of Distinction Among Them* (Kent State University Press, 1999), 185.
26. G. Michael Pratt, "The Battle of Fallen Timbers: An Eyewitness Perspective," *Northwest Ohio Quarterly* 67, no. 1 (Winter 1995): 4.
27. Interview with Sarah Munger, Draper Manuscripts, Series S, Vol. 20, pages 212–13, State Historical Society of Wisconsin, Madison. We will probably never be able to verify the story of Munger's death, but it is worth noting that at one point, mounted American dragoons engaged the Canadians, so it is very possible that a wounded Munger was killed by a saber blow from a mounted American.
28. John Graves Simcoe, *The Correspondence of Lieutenant Governor John Graves Simcoe: With Allied Documents Relating to His Administration of the Government of Upper Canada*, edited by E.A. Cruikshank (Ontario Historical Society, 1923). Available athttps://archive.org/stream/correspondencewi02simc/correspondencewi02simc_djvu.txt.

    The Essex and Kent Scottish Infantry Regiment is still in service today. They fought in the War of 1812, the Patriot War (1838), the South African War (1899–1900), World War I, World War II and, more recently, NATO missions in Egypt, Cyprus, Croatia, Bosnia, Afghanistan, Ukraine and Latvia.
29. Oliver M. Spencer, *The Indian Captivity of O. M. Spencer* (Legare Street Press, 2022), 88.
30. Robert S. Allen, "The British Indian Department and the Frontier in North America, 1755–1830," Canadian Historic Sites: Occasional Papers in Archaeology and History No. 14, http://parkscanadahistory.com.
31. Dictionary of Canadian Biography, "Elliott, Matthew," http://www.biographi.ca.
32. Reginald Horsman, *Matthew Elliott, British Indian Agent* (Wayne State University Press, 1964), 207.
33. Robert S. Allen, *The British Indian Department and the Frontier in North America, 1755–1830* National Historic Parks and Sites Branch, Parks Canada, Indian and Northern Affairs, 1975.

34. Simcoe, *Correspondence.*
35. Dictionary of Canadian Biography, "Caldwell, William," http://www.biographi.ca.
36. Eric Sterner, *The Battle of Upper Sandusky* (Westholme Publishing, 2023), 100.
37. Sugden, *Blue Jacket*, 34.
38. WikiTree, "William Charles Shortt (1764–1813)," https://www.wikitree.com.
39. Touring Ohio, "Fort Stephenson," http://touringohio.com.
40. Marilyn Wendler, *The Foot of the Rapids* (Daring Books, 1988), 172.
41. Mary Stockwell, *The Other Trail of Tears: The Removal of the Ohio Indians* (Westholme Publishing, 2014), 179.
42. Peter R DeMontravel, *A Hero to His Fighting Men* (Kent State University Press, 1998), 206.

Chapter 5

43. Captain Daniel Dobbins, the Dobbins Papers, Buffalo History Museum.
44. Benson J. Lossing, *Pictorial Field-Book of the War of 1812* (Firebird Press, 2003). Special thanks to Ken Dickson, who provided much of the research for this piece.
45. Wendler, *Foot of the Rapids*, 314.
46. Michael Carrick, "Trade Guns: Muskets of the Indian Trade," Discover Lewis & Clark, http://www.lewis-clark.org.
47. William A. Fox, "Dragon Sideplates from York Factory: A New Twist on an Old Tail," *Manitoba Archaeological Journal* 2, no. 2 (1992). Available at https://www.academia.edu/847109.
48. Richard Holt, "Pre-1814 Martial Contract Rifles," *Society of American Gun Collectors Bulletin* 47 (Fall 1982).
49. F. Clever Bald, "Fort Miamis, Outpost of Empire," *Northwest Ohio Quarterly* 16, no. 2 (1942).
50. Simcoe, *Correspondence.*
51. Simcoe, *Correspondence*, 405–08.
52. Steve Brown, "British Regiments and the Men Who Led Them 1793–1815," https://www.napoleon-series.org.
53. Louisa Charlotte Frampton, "Princess Charlotte and Mrs. Campbell" *Gentleman's Magazine* 17 (1876).
54. Dave Palmer, *1794: America, Its Army, and the Birth of the Nation* (Presidio Press, 1994), 32.
55. G. Michael Pratt, "The Battle of Fallen Timbers: An Eyewitness Perspective," *Northwest Ohio Quarterly* (Winter 1995): 4.
56. Thomas A. Chambers, *Memories of War: Visiting Battlegrounds and Bonefields in the Early American Republic* (Cornell University Press, 2012), 30.
57. Steven E. Anders, "With All Due Honors: A History of the Quartermaster Graves Registration Mission," *Quartermaster Professional Bulletin* (September 1988), Army Quartermaster Foundation, https://www.quartermasterfoundation.org.
58. According to Daryl Baldwin, foremost expert on the Miami language, most Miami (Myaamia) words end with the *ah* sound: the village, Ke ki on gAH; the people, MyaamiAH; the chief Pacanne, P koum kAH; the Chief Little Turtle, MihšihkinaahkwAH.
59. Heidelberg College turned the remains over to the Metroparks in 2018, and the process of repatriation in accordance with federal law was started.

ABOUT THE AUTHOR

Photo by Joan Felmlee.

Dave Westrick fell in love with Ohio history growing up on a farm in Northwest Ohio. He graduated from Ohio University with a degree in journalism. After a career in journalism and communications, he turned his attention to research, specializing in the early frontier era. He has written and lectured extensively on the Battle of Fallen Timbers. Dave serves on the boards of several history groups, including the Maumee Valley Historical Society, and is a former president of the Fallen Timbers Battlefield Preservation Committee. He lives with his wife, Nanci, in Maumee, Ohio.